GW01003487

SUSSEX
SCANDALS

RUPERT TAYLOR

With Illustrations by Don Osmond

COUNTRYSIDE BOOKS
NEWBURY, BERKSHIRE

COUNTRYSIDE BOOKS
3 CATHERINE ROAD
NEWBURY, BERKSHIRE

ISBN 0 905392 81 7

Produced through MRM (Print Consultants) Ltd., Reading
Typeset by Acorn Bookwork, Salisbury
Printed in England by J. W. Arrowsmith Ltd., Bristol

For Cloe and Daisy

Acknowledgement

With special thanks to Anne Hilton, John Eccles and Matt Tapp for their valuable assistance.

Rupert Taylor

CONTENTS

1

THE ACID BATH KILLER

'If I told you the truth you wouldn't believe me. It sounds too fantastic for belief.'

So John George Haigh told the police when confessing to the murder of Mrs Olive Durand-Deacon at his plastic finger nail factory at Crawley. It was a crime that shocked the nation through its sheer unpleasantness for Haigh also boasted: 'Mrs Durand-Deacon no longer exists. She has disappeared completely and no trace of her can ever be found . . . I have destroyed her with acid.'

All murders arouse interest, but there is nothing the Great British Public enjoys more than feeling queasy when reading the facts over the breakfast table. This had all the ingredients for popular press addicts to be deliciously horrified and for tender sensibilities to be offended, especially as Haigh admitted five similar crimes and claimed that before the destruction of the bodies he had drunk a glassful of every victim's blood. For the poor people of Crawley, trying to build a reputation for genteel respectability and healthy commerce in their new town in that spring of 1949, all the publicity was a disaster.

Small, dapper Mr Haigh, who had the gift of charming rich old ladies, was wrong when he asserted that no trace of Mrs Durand-Deacon remained, for it was the painstaking forensic work that played a key part in his ultimate conviction. He had met the portly 69-year-old at the Onslow Court Hotel in London and she rashly accepted an invitation to visit his factory in Sussex, which was in fact little more than a storehouse in Leopold Road containing three ten-gallon carboys of concentrated sulphuric acid.

It was there that he shot Mrs Durand-Deacon with his ·38 Enfield, removed her Persian lamb coat and jewellery and dumped her fully-clothed body into a 40-gallon tank before going for an egg on toast and a cup of tea at the cafe across the road. He returned to pump concentrated sulphuric acid into the tank, remembering that after 20 to 30 minutes the tank would become too hot to touch, and finally left for dinner at The George Hotel. Three days later he examined the tank and pumped in more acid, judging decomposition complete the following day when he pumped off the contents outside the storeroom.

His arrest and confession came a week later. A friend of the victim was worried by her disappearance after her rendezvous with Haigh and he volunteered to accompany her to the police, because he thought he 'might help'.

Police suspicions grew when they discovered that the man so anxious to give them a helping hand in their investigation had a criminal record for fraud and theft. They invited him to return to Chelsea Police Station after establishing that Mrs Durand-Deacon's jewellery had been sold to a shop in Horsham for £100 and a cleaner's receipt for her Persian lamb coat, dated the day after her disappearance, had been found at Haigh's storeroom, together with the acid, rubber protective clothing, a revolver and ammunition. He confessed, asking what his chances were of being released from Broadmoor. He also seemed to be under the misapprehension that because there was no body he could not be tried for murder.

The rough ground outside the storeroom was covered with pebbles, but there was one in particular that pathologist Professor Keith Simpson was looking for, taking into account the nature of the crime and the age and habits of the missing widow. He found what he was looking for almost immediately – a pebble about the size of a cherry with polished facets. Laboratory tests proved it to be a human gallstone. Embedded in a thick charred greasy substance were several pieces of eroded bone, the greater part of a left foot, and inside the green painted steel drum in which the body had been digested the professor saw a hairpin stuck in the grease at the bottom.

An area of yellowish sludge measuring six feet by four feet, and three to four inches deep, was dug up and packed into wooden boxes for patient sifting at the laboratory. Altogether some 475 lb of grease and earth were transported to Scotland Yard and from this the scientists were able to reconstruct the body of a person: an elderly, slightly arthritic woman with gallstones, who had false teeth of an unusual kind, a left foot that fitted a particular shoe, and who had been carrying a red plastic handbag with a lipstick container in it. From the amount of body fat discovered they knew that she was stoutly built.

In a celebrated trial at Lewes Assize Court, Haigh's defence counsel asked the jury for a verdict of guilty but insane. The prosecution said there was a perfectly rational explanation for all six murders, including the one for which he was tried – money. The jury took only eighteen minutes to make up its mind that Haigh was guilty and sane and he went to the gallows at Wandsworth Prison.

He had been too impatient. The bizarre nature of the case aroused considerable medical and scientific interest and there were a number of experiments which indicated that about a month of immersion would have destroyed all the exhibits that sent him to the rope – except the gallstone.

But Haigh had found notoriety; he wrote to his parents from prison: 'It isn't everybody who can create more sensation than a film star. Only Princess Margaret or Mr Churchill could command such interest.'

2

L OATHSOME LUST

'Young girls of gentle birth required to look after large dogs in the country; live in; experience unnecessary; commonsense essential.'

So read the advertisement in *The Times* in the early 1920s. An attractive prospect for those with a fondness for animals and the idea of a healthy, outdoor sort of life. Hundreds replied, but the chosen few found more than they had bargained for when they made their way to Pippingford Park, a large country estate on Ashdown Forest near Nutley. Their duties extended far beyond taking Fido for a walk and if they were inexperienced when they arrived they certainly were not when they left. These young girls of gentle birth were expected to gratify the urges of the master of the estate, Hayley Morriss, a 37-year-old gentleman of independent means with exotic but unspecific connections as a merchant in the Chinese trade. Aiding and abetting his wicked ways was his wife Madeleine, a one-time domestic servant who had also pursued a career on the stage.

The mysterious comings and goings at the Crow's Nest, an isolated house where the couple lived on the Pippingford Park estate, had not failed to attract the notice of the locals and the gossip and speculation was further fuelled by the revelations of would-be kennel maids. The law stepped in to put an end to the nocturnal pleasures of Mr Morriss and to protect other innocents from marching hopefully up the driveway through his 1,000 acres. Morriss and his wife found themselves standing arm in arm in the dock at Lewes Assizes to answer twenty-two counts of offences against young girls.

The *Sussex Express* report of that four day trial just before Christmas in 1925 did not seek to shock or titillate and was extremely coy about exactly what had been going on – no easy task in a story that spread itself over most of page eight and ran to nearly four thousand words. But the village and the surrounding neighbourhood had long before guessed the shocking set-up. The couple had been procuring girls for his pleasure and she had been a willing accomplice.

They pleaded not guilty but as the bizarre details emerged it became obvious that Morriss had taken advantage of the teenagers who replied to his advertisement. The facts were related 'with great distress' by some individuals as they gave evidence in court, but he seems to have had his fair share of headaches from the young ladies under his roof. It was implied that one intended to make Morriss pay dearly for what he had done to her: £1,000, in fact, and a new start in California. He had also instructed the sub-postmistress at Nutley, Ethel Whitewood, not to accept any telephone calls out of Pippingford Park unless they were made by a man. It seems the girls had been using the phone for their own purposes and had been running up large bills.

But his appetite was not blunted and Morriss even sought a little variety from girls who scanned the 'situations vacant' columns of *The Times*. He and his wife took a trip down to Brighton in their Rolls Royce, where they picked up an attractive couple of young women holidaying by the sea, who had been to a dance at the Regent. Mrs Morriss approached them first, introduced them to hubby and then they were driven back to Pippingford Park for dinner, during which they were offered situations on the estate by Morriss. It was an incident that led to an angry confrontation when the fiance of one of the girls called to demand an explanation. Morriss bluffed his way out of it by saying he thought the girls had been left in the lurch at Brighton without any money.

The evidence given by Sergeant Lister of Scotland Yard was clearly so distressing that Mrs Morriss, unwell before the trial began, collapsed in the dock. She was to collapse again when sentence was passed on her and had to be carried from the dock.

The judge, Mr Justice Avory, made his views plain on the case. Referring to an incident in which Morriss had said he had gone to the bedroom of one of the girls simply to say 'Goodnight', his lordship remarked: 'What is a man in this position, living in a house like this, doing going to say goodnight to a female servant in his employment?' Referring to the advertisement in *The Times*, he asked: 'Why young girls? Why are girls of gentle birth required to look after large dogs?' And the judge told the jury that when considering the case of Mrs Morriss 'you must not only draw the inference that she was actively engaged in aiding and abetting on these occasions, but that in engaging the girls as she did she must have been conspiring with Morriss, knowing what was going to happen'.

The jury took just twenty-seven minutes to return with 'guilty' verdicts and Judge Avory turned his indignant wrath on Morriss: 'The statute under which you have been convicted fixes a maximum punishment of two years, but in your case not only have you committed these offences upon these young girls under sixteen, but you have been convicted by the jury of pursuing a systematic course of procuring young girls and young women for the purpose of gratifying your loathsome lust at this house.' The judge felt the law provided a 'quite inadequate punishment'. He sentenced Morriss to three years in prison, two of them with hard labour, and added: '. . . as you have used your wealth for the purpose of ensnaring these girls into the position in which you could take advantage of them, it is only right that a portion of that wealth should go towards paying the costs of the prosecution. I order you to pay a sum not exceeding £1,000 towards the costs of the prosecution. Go down.' And Morriss did.

Mrs Morriss received a little more leniency, because she had acted 'under the influence if not the coercion' of her husband, but her part was 'a most disgusting one for any woman to have played'. She got nine months with hard labour. The couple appealed two months later, but this was rejected.

The scandal caused some alarm in high places. Henry Cowan MP and Lady Cowan lived at a house near Uckfield also known as the Crow's Nest. As it was only about three miles from the house where the dirty deeds took place they had found the case particularly distressing and a statement was read to the court disassociating the honourable member and his wife from any connection with the other Crow's Nest.

3

THE KISS

The good people of Lewes confused art with obscenity when they had the chance to make Rodin's priceless statue *The Kiss* a part of the cultural heritage of the town. The famous sculpture, showing a naked couple locked in embrace, was placed in Lewes Town Hall on permanent loan in 1913.

But the local population took exception to its mild eroticism. It was circled by railings to stop anyone getting too close and finally a sheet was placed over the sculpture to preserve the town's morality. The town hall was used for boxing matches in those days and on one particularly popular night many of the watching crowd climbed onto the precious work of art to get a better view. In the end its donor, Edward Perry Warren, was asked in no uncertain terms to take the statue back. It was placed in the coach house at Lewes House, where Warren lived, and there it remained out of sight until his death.

There is every reason to believe that had Lewes taken *The Kiss* (*Le Baiser*) to its heart, Warren would have given the statue to the town in perpetuity. Today the same statue stands in the Tate Gallery in London where no-one can even begin to guess at its value.

Warren, known as the 'mad millionaire', was an amazing man. He drank at the old Bear Hotel with his like-minded male friends, who more often than not wore Arab clothes and conversed in classical Greek over their pints.

He was happy roaming the Downs on horseback or canoeing on the river Ouse with his cronies, seeing Lewes as a safe haven after journeys to the East in search of antiquities. An exceptionally rich American – he also owned Shelleys and School Hill House in Lewes – he bought priceless antiques and modern works of art for his own enjoyment and for museums in America and Britain.

Lewes House was hardly an American's dream country home, but Warren liked its large north-facing rooms which he could fill with vases and busts. It also had a south-facing garden which gave privacy and light and colour. The horrors of the First World War brought out the practical side to his nature when he ran the School Hill House Military Hospital at his own expense.

Warren had ordered *Le Baiser* direct from Rodin himself. It cost 25,000 old francs and that included the marble. The pair had met in 1903 when Rodin came to Lewes and apparently the famous sculptor and the gifted collector did not quite see eye to eye. Warren went into raptures over Greek marbles and bronzes while Rodin, a creative artist first and foremost, said: 'Let me go out into the street and stop the first person I meet; I will make a work of art from him.' Unfortunately Rodin did not step out into School Hill, denying some passing local the chance of being immortalised in stone.

To the modern mind the scandal lies not in the erotic nature of the man and woman so carefully chiselled out but in the fact that the town coldly rejected a treasure. Former mayor, Frank Mayhew, recalled seeing the statue in drapes at Lewes House as a boy of ten. 'I can remember my father being furious that the borough council couldn't see the beauty of the statue,' he said. 'It looked colossal to me but I can't remember being shocked at its nudity. It's a tragedy it is not still in Lewes. It just wasn't appreciated at the time.'

There is no record that Warren was upset in any way that Lewes rejected his statue. Perhaps he expected it. When he died in 1928 the contents of his house, including

The Kiss, were put up for sale by Gorringes. Graham Gorringe, son of Rowland who conducted the auction, recalled: 'It was our first major sale. There was some incredible stuff there. It was our sale of the century. But *The Kiss* didn't meet our reserve of £9,000. It simply wasn't a sought-after piece at the time and just moving it was an enormous task.'

The sculpture was bought privately by Warren's friend H. Asa-Thomas who lived at Shelleys and later at Bineham House, Chailey (which is now demolished). He later gave it to his daughter, Mrs Pamela Tremlett, and in 1939 she in turn gave *The Kiss* on loan to the Tate. In 1955 the museum bought the sculpture from her for a nominal £7,500. It now has pride of place at the Tate but few people in Lewes realise that it is the same statue that once stood in their Town Hall.

Controversy over carving was to repeat itself some sixty years after the town kissed goodbye to Rodin. A large and expensive sculpture was erected in the middle of a roundabout at the entrance to the new South Street Tunnel. The subject matter again caused offence – only this time the populace was wondering what it was supposed to be. A giant ammonite, they were told. Apparently the local geologist Gideon Mantell used ammonites to adorn the capitals of his house in the High Street. The sculpture is still there and has been taken to local hearts. It is affectionately called 'Brian the Snail'.

4

FIVE YEARS OF HELL

There can be some unholy rows when a clergyman and his flock fall out. Rightly or wrongly, men of the cloth are expected to be of unimpeachable character and behaviour, so it is a recipe for bitterness when they fall short of the standards expected of them by lesser mortals.

Nothing has been quite as bitter in Sussex as the devastating effect the Rev. Edward Fitzgerald Synnot MA had upon the picturesque village of Rusper. It was an unlikely combination to begin with. He was a blunt Irishman with forthright views, some tough city parishes left tamed in his wake and the reputation for being something of a boxer who would not hesitate to use his pugilistic talents if the need arose. The parish he came to during the years of the First World War was quiet and highly respectable, a place which has been lovingly described as 'a village that has just stood still'.

It did not take long for the new rector and his parishioners to cease seeing eye to eye. He was on a meagre living of £280 a year so supplemented this (and helped the British war effort) by becoming something of a farmer in his spare time. Cow stalls at the rectory might have been acceptable, but muddy wellies in the church of St Mary Magdalene when he was taking Communion was not. Neither were his bluff and outspoken views in the pulpit or in the village street. Perhaps it was his previous experiences in London's East End that made the man who bore a remarkable physical resemblance to Ulster's Rev. Ian Paisley particularly abrasive to the Rusper gentry.

But he had his supporters, especially among the poorer folk, and a great wedge was driven through the village – you were either pro or anti Synnott. Parochial Church Council meetings to discuss the situation and try and heal the rift ended in uproar, with inkpots and even bricks used as missiles by furious locals against each other. There were dark rumours of assault and skirt-chasing by the rector and things took a decidedly nasty turn when Mr Synnott received a package through the post. It contained the tail of his pet dog.

The rector then made the extraordinary move of airing the Rusper rumpus to a wider audience in the form of a book about his experiences. It is today a rare collector's piece but when it first appeared in 1920 more than a few copies would have found their way into the fireplace in disgust. The title was *Five Years Hell in a Country Parish* by the Rector of Rusper.

Not a title to spread peace and understanding. The content, too, pulled no punches though he wrote that he bore malice to no man and stressed that only 'after the most careful deliberation have I decided to tell the whole world my remarkable story'. It was supposed to be a sort of warning to other clergymen on how to avoid the sorrows Mr Synnott, his wife and daughter had shared and included descriptions 'in all their terrible realism of some of the agonising experiences through which I have passed'.

A sample of the introduction to this little bombshell gives a good indication of its contents. Mr Synnott wrote: 'When I accepted the living of this tiny parish of Rusper, friends assured me that after twelve years of strenuous work in the church I deserved the passive life I was about to enjoy. That was five years ago. Five terrible years! How often during those five years of agony have I wished that instead of coming to a quiet country parish I had declined the living and pursued the harder, more strenuous life of which I had been accustomed.'

Beware of rosy pictures painted by friends of a beautiful rectory over which golden honeysuckle climbed, Mr Synnott advised grimly. Beware of the ideal of good-hearted rustics who greeted their rector with a doff of the cap or a curtsey, welcoming him as a friend, guide and minister. Beware, too, of happy thoughts of composing sermons in God's green fields and leafy lanes instead of the flickering gaslight of a London slum.

The vision had been very different from reality, he moaned. 'When Queen Mary died she spoke of Calais being engraved on her heart. When I die I think the name of Rusper will be found eaten deep into mine.'

His introduction concluded: 'I will show how the idle and thoughtless tittle-tattle of a small village can grow and spread until the first feeble untruth in which it begins assumes a shape so ugly and alarming that the life of a village priest becomes a burden almost unbearable.

'I will show how every mannerism, every gesture, every modern thought, every unusual word or act of a man with an up-to-date and original mind; every suggestion of muscular Christianity which would pass unnoticed in a town or city or be counted to him for righteousness can be made the subject of village gossip and criticism leading to the ruin of the rector and his family.'

And show them he did! On the pages that followed, the good-hearted rustics he had been told to expect were portrayed in reality as narrow as well as dirty-minded, with un-Christian values and loud mouths.

But perhaps the most wounding line amongst them all (at least for half the village population) was Mr Synnott's caustic remark: 'No Helens of Troy in Rusper – a plainer lot of women I have never seen.'

All hell broke loose when the book appeared. The anti-Synnott brigade said he had gone way over the mark and would have to be got rid of – but the only way of doing so was to have him unfrocked. Consequently, he was hauled before an ecclesiastical court to explain allegations from the Rusper flock that he had been misbehaving himself with the choirgirls. Synnott was cleared, and made the most of it. On his return he was met at Faygate station by the Crawley Silver Band and escorted back to his village in musical triumph.

He was a bear-cat for nerve. Despite 'five years of hell' he stayed on in the village he had derided so heartily for a good many more and is remembered to this day by some older villagers for the kindness beneath the rugged exterior. He finally left for a new parish in Kent in 1932, but was invited back by his successor, the Rev. Hugh Trevaskis, to preach the sermon one Sunday. Significantly, the church was packed that day.

5
PRICE OF MUTINY

The soldiers of the Oxfordshire Militia Regiment were lagging a little on their long march over the Downs. The drums and fifes began to play *Brighton Camp* and the long line of men was instantly braced, the step picked up and the weary faces became brighter. Some began to whistle the tune and it was not long before the words were being roared out:

> 'But now I'm bound for Brighton Camp,
> Kind Heaven then pray guide me,
> And send me safe back home again
> To the girl I've left behind me.'

Despite this sudden uplift in spirits, they were not a happy body of men in their stiff uniforms on this spring day in 1795. They were on their way to Blatchington Barracks, near Seaford, as part of the annual military manoeuvres in Sussex which involved many thousands of men, regular soldiers and the militia corps, as Britain looked uneasily across the Channel at the threat posed by the new Republic of France.

The Oxfordshire Militia had a grievance at the bad quality of the bread and flour which they were served and the prices charged for them. The angry murmurs and mutterings increased until the men were in a condition ripe for mutiny. They merely required a leader to undertake any devilry. One was soon found and on a Friday

morning in April some five hundred men left Blatchington Barracks with fixed bayonets and marched to Seaford, where they seized all the flour, bread and meat they
could find and sold it at below current prices. One of the
officers, Captain Harben, exhorted the disaffected men to
return to their duty. He promised he would buy the loads
of wheat himself and then retail it to them at £4 a load
less than it should cost him. His offer was received with
cheers and the majority seemed inclined to accept it and
disperse. But they were dissuaded by some of the more
desperate, who said they were more likely to secure the
end they had in view by carrying out their own plans.

From Seaford the mutineers proceeded to the tide-mill
at Bishopstone where they found a considerable quantity
of wheat and flour which they prepared to convey under
escort to Seaford. They seized wagons and horses from
the neighbouring farm and loaded the vehicles with
about two hundred sacks of grain. They next compelled
some men who were loading a sloop with flour from the
tide-mill to work her down to Newhaven, to which they
then marched, took possession of the town, and helped
themselves to such goods as took their fancy. The sailors
were then ordered to unload the three hundred sacks of
flour from the sloop and place it in a warehouse. The
soldiers mounted a guard on the flour and it was sold to
anyone who cared to purchase it at fifteen shillings a
sack. The majority of the men later returned peacefully
to their barracks, but about sixty remained in the town
and they soon became exceedingly drunk and riotous.

News of the mutineers quickly reached the authorities
and the Lancashire Fencibles from Brighton and some
Horse Artillery, stationed at Lewes, marched with two
field pieces on Newhaven. They were met by a body of
mutineers who, though they had no ammunition, formed
up with the intention of contesting the advance. The
cannons crashed out and the mutineers were over-
powered and disarmed after a mêlée in which men from
both sides were wounded. Twenty-five prisoners were

23

taken to Lewes and lodged at the House of Correction and the remainder were marched back to Blatchington and placed under guard by a troop of Fencibles. Most of the soldiers faced charges of felony. But a handful were suddenly to realise that their impulsive action rendered them 'capitally punishable by martial law'.

James Sykes and William Sampson, militiamen said to be of respectable character, were sentenced to death by hanging. Sykes was charged with taking part in the riot at Bishopstone, and with stealing ten hempen sacks and fifty bushels of flour, the property of Thomas Barton and Edmund Catt (the proprietor of the tide-mill); the charge against Sampson was that of stealing three bottles of rum, several sacks, and a quantity of flour with a total value of £10. The death sentence hinged on the evidence of a witness who declared that he had heard one of the prisoners say that if Mr Catt had been present at the time his property was taken his body 'would have been as stuck as full of bayonets as it would hold'. This proved an intention to murder, said the court, and Sykes and Sampson were removed to Horsham Jail to await execution.

A day or two later thirteen more of the mutineers faced a General Court Martial at the Castle Tavern in Brighton. The trial occupied eight days and ended in Private Edward Cooke – popularly called 'Captain Cook' because he led the mutineers – and Private Henry Parish being found guilty and sentenced to be shot. Six others were sentenced to be flogged, one to receive 1,500 lashes, one 500 and the remaining four 1,000 each. Another of the rebels condemned to death had his sentence commuted afterwards to transportation to Botany Bay. Four others were liberated.

The terrible sentences passed upon the chief mutineers, especially upon Cooke and Parish who were both young and headstrong, caused revulsion among the public. The inhabitants showed the men sympathy during the trial as they were marched each day under escort from the guardhouse to the Castle Tavern and back.

Every night and morning residents of Russell Street took provisions to the unhappy men, which were passed through the bars of their airing ground. A petition promoted by the residents of Brighton in favour of a reprieve was declined.

Goldstone Bottom near Hove was the site chosen as the scene of execution. Today it is the home of Brighton and Hove Albion Football Club, but at the end of the 18th century it was out in the country, a sparsely populated valley of the Downs. Before dawn on the morning of June 13th the Oxfordshire Militia – the regiment to which the condemned men belonged – was on the march from Blatchington to Brighton. It was from their own regiment that the executioners of Cooke and Parish were chosen and at 4 a.m. they received their own comrades as prisoners and escorted them in an open cart to Goldstone Bottom.

All the troops encamped at Brighton, some thirteen regiments, were drawn up in a hollow square about half a mile in length. First came the floggings, with three of the men receiving a hundred lashes each before the surgeon in attendance said that as a consequence of their imprisonment they could take no more at that time. The other three were forgiven their sentence, mercy so unexpected that one of them fell on his knees before the general to thank him.

There was no reprieve for Cooke and Parish, though. They were marched along the line of troops and must have noticed the artillerymen with lighted matches and loaded guns ready to snuff out the slightest hint of trouble if there were still mutinous ideas among the troops. On the heights above were assembled two thousand cavalry and a number of civilian spectators.

The men were ordered to kneel on their own coffins and face the firing platoon of twelve men six paces away. They then exchanged a few words with each other and with the chaplain, the Rev. Mr Dring. The clergyman was of an extremely nervous nature and, having a great

25

horror of the duty he had been called upon to perform, had previously asked that having administered the last rites to the condemned men he should be given an opportunity to get beyond the report of the volley before the order to fire was given. This was agreed, but unfortunately he had not gone many paces when the command 'fire' rang out. Such was the effect on the chaplain that he fell swooning to the ground and never recovered from the shock. Poor Parish was not killed outright by the volley and one of the platoon, detailed to hold his fire in case of mishap, ran forward, placed his musket at the prisoner's ear and pulled the trigger.

The assembled troops were re-formed and, led by the Oxfordshire Militia, were marched past the bodies as a salutary lesson. So great an impression was made upon the regiment of the mutineers that many of the men wept. Cooke and Parish were buried in Hove Churchyard, but at the spot where the execution had taken place a shepherd cut the shape of two coffins in the turf and marked the position of the firing party in a similar manner. For half a century these marks were visited by the curious until eventually they were obliterated by the plough.

Privates Sykes and Sampson, who were condemned to die on the scaffold for their part in the riot, met their fate at Horsham. From the scaffold they called upon the assembled crowd of spectators outside the prison to shun drunkenness and mobs. Two hangmen from the Old Bailey attended to carry out the demand of the law. One of them bungled his job, carelessly taking Sampson's hair into the noose, and death came slowly to the unfortunate soldier.

6

THE SQUIRE WHO WENT TO JAIL

When Horatio Bottomley was released from prison in 1927 he was a disgraced charlatan whose name had become indelibly linked in the minds of the British public with fraud and shady dealing. Five years behind bars had been the punishment of the court for the swindler and he might have expected to be shunned by society when he came out.

But in the slice of Sussex he had made his own he was given a hero's welcome. The whole population of Upper Dicker turned out for his homecoming in a colourful reception that was more than just a feudal sense of duty towards the squire. Bottomley was held in genuine affection by the country folk, and it is a feeling that persists more than half a century after his death among those who remember him. The older generation in Upper Dicker recall the kind and generous man who built many of the comfortable cottages in the village, livened-up rural life with the lavish parties he threw at the grand home he built for himself, knew everyone by name and made patriotic speeches at the village school.

Bottomley's was the classic rags to riches story. He was at one time tipped as a future Prime Minister, a man dubbed both the 'Napoleon of Finance' and 'the greatest crook in England', whose silver tongue and grandiose swindles raised him to dizzy heights. His meteoric career began when he ran away from an orphanage at the age of fourteen in 1874 to become an errand boy at a London solicitor's office and later a shorthand writer in the Supreme Court of Judicature. In 1880 he married Eliza Norton, the daughter of a Battersea debt collector, and they settled in Clapham where Bottomley became in public a pillar of the Methodist Church and in private a virulent atheist.

He went into the printing business and in 1884 started the *Hackney Hansard*. The success of this small suburban weekly prompted him to publish others and led to the Hansard Publishing Union. It crashed in 1891, leaving him bankrupt and facing a charge of conspiracy to defraud. He defended himself in court with such eloquence that he was acquitted, and was advised that his talents as an orator would make him an ideal lawyer.

Instead, Bottomley plunged audaciously into the world of finance, founding the Joint Stock Trust and Institute and floating a number of Australian gold-mining companies and other enterprises (including the appropriately named Nil Desperandum Mines), few of which paid the shareholders and most of which were phoney. Despite this, and the fact that between 1901 and 1905 sixty-seven bankruptcy petitions and writs were filed against him, he amassed a fortune – enough to feature in a *Financial Times* series 'Men of Millions'. It was estimated he made £3,000,000 by promoting nearly fifty different companies.

The one-time orphan and pen-pusher was not loathe to part with his cash and saw Upper Dicker as the perfect rural haven away from the cares of the business world. He built himself a mansion called The Dicker, and threw himself into the role of country squire. The Dicker was the only house in the village with a telephone but he allowed everyone to use it. He became the generous president of Dicker Cricket Club and established a highly successful racehorse stables. But his winnings on the Cesarewitch, the Steward's Cup and other prizes of the turf were largely squandered on gambling, a collection of

mistresses in London, theatrical enterprises, extravagant entertaining and gifts.

The money kept rolling in, though. Bottomley bought the *Sun* in 1898 and founded *John Bull* in 1906. He was engaged to write for the *Sunday Pictorial* for the fabulous sum at the turn of the century of £100 an article, and took on others to write them for him at a quarter of the fee.

He was elected Liberal MP for South Hackney in 1906, a position soured a year later when the shareholders of the Joint Stock Trust petitioned for its liquidation and an eighteen-month long examination was made of his books, of which the important ones were missing. He was charged with fraud at the Guildhall in 1909 but his skill and wit in court secured an acquittal. The outbreak of the First World War in 1914 saw Bottomley vow to be a reformed character and break with his 'sordid past'. It may have had a lot to do with another declaration of bankruptcy, though he had been making large sums through rigged lotteries and sweepstakes.

The war years saw him in a new role: 'the country's recruiting sergeant' whose patriotic speeches (for which he took a fee) and jingoistic ranting in the mass circulation *John Bull* made him a national hero. He regained his seat at South Hackney, this time as an independent, with a massive majority. But the crash was not far away and it came with the infamous Victory Bond fraud in 1919. Suspicion about his activities grew and though outwardly he blustered that 50,000 ex-servicemen would march on Westminster if any attempt were made to prosecute him, privately he confessed to a friend: 'I have been sitting on a keg of gunpowder for years and it might go up at any moment.'

A receiver was appointed to examine his enterprises and in March 1922 he was charged with fraudulent conversion and was committed for trial at the Old Bailey. In May, amid a blaze of publicity, he was found guilty on twenty-three counts out of twenty-four and sentenced to seven years in prison. His appeal was rejected and he was formally expelled from the House of Commons in August. The prison sentence stunned his adopted county but most of all Bottomley himself, who had bought tickets for an Epsom race meeting in anticipation of wriggling out of trouble again. At Wormwood Scrubs they could not find a uniform big enough to fit the short, 17-stone convict and he found life behind bars particularly harrowing after his decades of the good life.

Shortly before his release in 1927 a *Daily Sketch* reporter went to Upper Dicker to find out how the village was reacting to the impending release of its squire. 'Bottomley was Dicker, and Dicker without him has been a sad place', said Mrs Prevett, the stationmaster's daughter. 'Dicker has gone to pieces since Bottomley went away.' Villagers revealed their plans to deck the place with banners and bunting, and engage the Hailsham Prize Band to welcome him home. Some of the men declared they would go to Berwick station and drag his car home in triumph. On a wider scale, his freedom was greeted with enthusiasm. A verse from a music-hall song ran:

> 'Then welcome home to Bottomley,
> Deny it if you can,
> He played his part; he's right at heart
> And every inch a man.'

Others believed the great con-man deserved his come-uppance. Bottomley, always a great name dropper, told a doctor friend as he hurried off to see a patient, Sir Douglas Hogg at Hailsham, 'give my love to Douglas'. The message was rather naively passed on and Sir Douglas (later to become Lord Hailsham) was furious. 'How dare that scoundrel send me a message?' he demanded.

The jaunty confidence and sharp wits of Bottomley had deserted him. He retired to The Dicker, glittering symbol of his heyday, to lick his wounds. The failure of a new weekly, *John Blunt*, in 1928 and the death of his loyal wife in 1930 broke him.

The man who once held audiences of thousands spellbound with his speeches in Trafalgar Square was reduced to a pathetic figure appearing on the stage to tell his life story and to applying, unsuccessfully, for an old age pension. He died, poor and in obscurity, on May 26th, 1933. His ashes were scattered on the Downland gallops he loved above the village of Alfriston, and his mansion is now a school.

7

THE CRUMBLES MURDER

Miss Ethel Duncan would surely have politely refused Patrick Mahon's invitation to a weekend of fun if she had any inkling of what the seaside bungalow contained. In the bedroom next door to the one in which she was entertained by Mr Mahon was a cabin trunk containing a dismembered body. The woman now lying in pieces inside the trunk had been cavorting in the same bed as typist Miss Duncan only two or three nights before.

Miss Duncan escaped the grisly fate of the previous guest that Easter of 1924 and the crime only came to light because Mrs Mahon had become suspicious about the activities of her philanderer husband. She had alerted the police after finding a cloakroom ticket in one of her husband's pockets. The police presented it at the left luggage department at Waterloo Station and were given a bag which, when prised open, was found to contain articles of women's silk underclothing, which appeared to be bloodstained, and a knife. The police put the bag back and lay in wait for whoever should come to claim it. Soon after six o'clock that evening Patrick Mahon, using the name Waller, presented the ticket and was invited by Detective Chief Inspector Percy Savage to accompany him to Scotland Yard. The contents of the bag were turned out: a torn pair of silk bloomers, two pieces of new white silk, a blue silk scarf and a large cook's knife, all stained with blood and grease. There was also a brown canvas racket bag with the initials 'E.B.K.'. Mahon, dressed in a well-made brown suit, his brown curly hair tinged with grey, said: 'I'm fond of dogs. I suppose I've carried home meat for dogs in it.'

This explanation did not satisfy Savage, who waited with patience until 11 o'clock when Mahon calmly described a 10-month affair with a woman who worked as a clerk in the City, of four days together at a bungalow near Eastbourne which ended in a violent quarrel in which he was hit a glancing blow with an axe and she was fatally injured after her head fell against an iron coal scuttle. In his panic, Mahon told the inspector, he had bought a knife and a saw and severed the woman's legs and head and stuffed the various parts into a trunk.

Still in the level, well-spoken voice he described how he later returned to the bungalow from London and burned the head, feet and legs in the sitting room grate. Later again, he returned to cut up the torso and arms, boiling some in a large pot at the bungalow and wrapping up smaller portions in brown paper and throwing them out of trains. Some of the flesh had been wrapped in the bloodstained clothing found in the bag. At the end of his macabre statement, albeit not an unreasonable defence against premeditated murder, he finally gave the name of the dead woman: Emily Beilby Kaye, single, aged twenty-nine and well educated.

Police went straight to the bungalow, standing on a lonely windswept stretch of shingle between Eastbourne and Pevensey Bay known as The Crumbles. The building was called the Officer's House because it had previously been the home of the officer in charge of the coastguard station. There were roses round the door but when police went inside the stench was almost unbearable. The scene, too, was ghastly. There were burned bones in the grates of the dining room and sitting room; a saucepan and a bath in the scullery contained human remains that had been boiled; in a bedroom was a bloodstained saw; in a trunk, marked with the initials 'E.B.K.', were portions of a woman's body; and in a biscuit tin were the heart and other internal organs. The atmosphere inside was so dreadful that detectives set up a table in the garden to work on. Police and pathologists found practically the whole body of the victim, a woman probably in an early state of pregnancy with nothing to indicate a natural death.

Mahon was 34 and worked as a salesman. He was notorious as a womaniser with a string of love affairs behind him. In 1916 he had been jailed for breaking into a bank and stunning a maidservant with a hammer (he had waited for her to regain consciousness then kissed and fondled her, begging forgiveness for the attack). His wife was the forgiving kind and when he had finished his sentence she recommended him for his job with the firm where she worked at Sunbury.

Emily Kaye was in fact thirty-four and had worked as a shorthand-typist in the City. She had soon succumbed to Mahon's blandishments and they began going out together. Early in 1924 she knew she was pregnant. He had made no secret of the fact he was married, but gave her a diamond and sapphire engagement ring and promised to take her to South Africa. On the strength of this she told all her friends what was planned and on April 7th gave up her room at Guilford Street, Bloomsbury.

Police discovered Mahon had bought the knife and saw three days before the alleged quarrel that led to the tragedy, and that Emily Kaye had given most of her £600 savings to her lover – money cashed before and after her death, the notes endorsed on each occasion with a false name and address. Murder, not an accident, was the line of the police investigation. Mahon had fleeced the woman who loved him and knew that if the child was born he would be exposed. So he rented the seaside bungalow at The Crumbles under the name Waller and arranged for Miss Kaye to stay with him there. Police never established exactly when he killed her, but it must have been soon after she wrote a last letter to a friend describing her happiness and future travels. She believed she was going to Cape Town to get married.

Before travelling to The Crumbles to keep his fateful appointment with Miss Kaye, Mahon had met Miss Ethel Duncan while walking in Richmond and it is some measure of the charm of the man that on the strength of a casual conversation in the street she had agreed to have dinner with him. They dined at a restaurant in Victoria – possibly on the very day he had killed Emily – and she agreed to spend the Easter holiday with him 'at a friend's bungalow at Eastbourne'. She arrived on Good Friday, was taken on a motoring tour of Sussex by Mahon, wined and dined and then taken to the bungalow. He was quite normal and in good spirits, she revealed, and she had a fleeting glimpse of the cabin trunk which he told her was used by the friend who owned the property to safeguard valuable books.

Mahon seems to have quickly tired of Miss Duncan. He left her to her own devices in Eastbourne on Saturday while he went to the races at Plumpton (where police believe he changed another of Emily's £100 notes) and sent himself a telegram saying he was required back at the office urgently. He returned to London with Miss Duncan so he could answer the bogus summons.

He then returned to The Crumbles and worked furiously over the next few days at disposing of the body. But for the incriminating contents of the bag at the left luggage cloakroom and the suspicions of his long-suffering wife he might have got away with it. There was nothing to connect Waller of the bungalow with Mahon, the salesman from Kew; and Miss Kaye would not have been reported missing because friends believed she had settled happily in South Africa.

Mahon maintained his smooth style at Lewes Assizes, wearing a specially ordered blue suit. His face was tanned (rumour had it with tobacco juice) and his hands carefully manicured. Only at the end did his composure crack when, under a merciless cross-examination from

35

Sir Henry Curtis Bennett, he sobbed into a silk handkerchief.

There was an eerie twist in the courtroom when a storm broke out as he was describing the gruesome events at Eastbourne. Mahon went white despite his tan as he recalled the storm on the night he put Emily Kaye's head in the fire – her hair had blazed, her eyes had opened in the heat and at that moment there was a tremendous clap of thunder, and lightning played around the room. He had run out in terror. His story that the death had been an accident was dismissed and Mahon went to the gallows on September 9th for 'one of the foulest crimes which has been committed in recent years'.

It was a scandalous crime that was the talk of Sussex in the 1920s and no doubt made more than one young lady a little uneasy about romantic idylls beside the breakers. But perhaps the biggest scandal was the ghoulish fascination The Crumbles held for many years afterwards. It had begun when police were making their sickening discoveries in the little house of horror as hundreds of local people tried to peer over the garden fence to get a view. Later, the Officer's House would be surrounded by stalls and booths to cater for the holidaymakers who flocked to see 'the place where it had all happened'. Violent death and its aftermath became a tourist attraction.

The bungalow has been demolished now but The Crumbles is still a place heavy in forbidding atmosphere. Haunted, some say, by the ghost of the unfortunate Emily Kaye.

8

THE HASTINGS RARITIES

Birds, particularly stuffed and mounted ones, are an unlikely source of controversy. But 23 years after his death a shy, mild-mannered old man from Hastings was at the centre of a scandal that rocked the ornithological world and is still a source of heated debate among the experts who study our feathered friends.

George Bristow died in 1939. He was a retiring character with old fashioned ways who worked as a taxidermist and gunsmith in a musty shop in Silchester Road, always wearing a white bib apron. His output of stuffed birds and beasts was by all accounts prolific in an era when the Victorian craze for taxidermy and rural memorabilia was on the decline. This may have prompted him to ginger-up interest in a dying art and led to the strange case of the Hastings Rarities.

It was in the mid 1950s that two eminent ornithologists, Edward Nicholson and James Ferguson-Lees, paid a visit to a museum in Hull and were surprised at the number of rare bird exhibits which emanated from Hastings and its environs. Surprise grew to suspicion when further investigations showed them that all the rather sorrowful collection frozen in lifelike poses had passed through Bristow's hands. 'An elaborate hoax', they cried, and put forward the theory that the small time businessman had been having birds specially brought in from Europe by returning sailors, weaving his magic with the stuffing and glass eyes and then passing them off as indigenous specie.

Their scepticism gathered momentum and in an unprecedented move in 1962 a complete edition of the august ornithological journal *British Birds* was taken up with an analysis of the evidence. This in turn found its way into the newspapers and the rarities scandal made headlines across the world. As a result some twenty species were ignominiously struck from the List of British Birds and doubt was cast on scores of others – the result of almost forty years of work by Bristow.

It was established that as early as 1916 the flow of rare birds 'discovered' in the Hastings area and immortalised by the man in the white bib apron had risen to such a degree that the editor of *British Birds*, H. J. Witherby, had grown more than a little anxious and had written to Bristow asking for further details. The request was never satisfactorily answered, but in a later letter Bristow protested innocence of any shady dealing: 'I have been told that the idea is I have birds sent over frozen,' he wrote, 'but this is preposterous; could I possibly get captains of ships or other officers to bother themselves over these little things? Even if I could it would have been found out years ago.'

Did he set out to trick people? If so, he could hardly have hoped to make money by doing so because stuffed birds, even rare and unusual ones, would only have made a few shillings from museums and people no longer wanted them adorning their mantelpieces. Fame or recognition were also unlikely motives for a man whose retiring nature was a byword in Hastings and who was always content to take a back seat.

The belief that Bristow was guiltless is still a strong one in his home town. The majority of his finds were authenticated by local natural historians of repute, and it is maintained that if there had been any chicanery on Bristow's part it might have been a little illicit trade in guns for poachers, not phoney birds.

The truth behind the rarities will probably never be known. But recent years have seen a reinstatement to the List of British birds of some of those dismissed as fakes, following the discovery of other examples on southern beaches. The purists are satisfied. So, presumably, would have been the quiet man from Hastings who never lived to know the rumpus his passion had caused.

9
DEATH AND THE DOCTOR

The *Daily Mail* summed up the whole bizarre story neatly: 'To shock Eastbourne is unfair; it's like booting an old lady as she sleeps in the armchair of memories.'

The report appeared before the murder trial that rocked the sedate seaside resort to its blue-rinsed roots in 1956, the culmination of years of gossip with the tongues clacking louder in the tea rooms every time a wealthy woman died.

The man at the centre of the gossip, rumour and finally murder investigation was Doctor John Bodkin Adams, MD, DA, D.Ph., of Kent Lodge, Trinity Trees, Eastbourne. He was an Ulsterman with a devout Christian upbringing, who had established himself as the most fashionable doctor in the town and who ranked himself not only as doctor but also friend and adviser to some of the best-known and most influential families in East Sussex. In the early 1950s he was making £7,000 a year from his practice and indulged his passion for cars by at one time owning five, two of them Rolls-Royces. A large man in every way, who pushed the scales over 17 stones, his horn-rimmed rounded spectacles appearing too small in their setting of a pink, fleshy face; a man who conducted Bible classes on Sunday afternoons and instructed the Young Crusaders, who worshipped with the Plymouth Brethren and was joint chairman of the YMCA.

Most of his patients were private, fee-paying clients and his hearty bedside manner made him a favourite with the lonely, wealthy old ladies in this retirement haven who made up such a high percentage of his register. He was bald and middle-aged, a confirmed bachelor who still maintained a friendly relationship with the girl he had hoped to marry in younger days, fond of chocolates and shooting, Savile Row suits and bridge. He appeared not to know about the ugly talk of jumble sales and cocktail parties – that every time one of his patients died he was left cash or goods. And the rate at which they died after changing their wills had become alarming.

The innuendo had begun before the Second World War, but it was the death of two elderly spinster sisters, Hilda and Clara Neil-Miller, that brought the doctor to the attention of Superintendent Herbert William Walter Hannam, known to his colleagues as 'The Count', and Detective-Sergeant Charles Hewitt, both of Scotland Yard's Murder Squad. What interested them was a bequest to the Neil-Miller's doctor, John Bodkin Adams, which amounted in 1954 to almost £5,000. The same doctor had benefited from many other one-time patients over the years, enjoying cash bequests alone totalling £45,000 together with gifts of cars, jewellery, silver and antiques. He had been named as a beneficiary in more than 132 wills, some of them long standing but more often of recent compilation. A witness stated that Clara Neil-Miller had been visited by Adams and left with her bedclothes thrown back and the windows flung open on a bitterly cold night. She had died the following day, not of coronary thrombosis as recorded by Adams on the death certificate, but of pneumonia, as an examination of the exhumed body revealed. The past cases of the good doctor came under intense scrutiny.

In 1956 Gertrude 'Bobbie' Hullett, a vivacious woman of only 49, died after four months of being treated constantly with sleeping drugs by Adams. At the end she was a staggering wreck, but two days before falling into a fatal coma she made out a cheque to Adams. In her will she left him a Rolls Royce. The inquest recorded a verdict of suicide and the doctor was severely reprimanded by the coroner for his diagnosis and treatment during Mrs Hullett's last days.

Superintendent Hannam's dossier of suspicious deaths was a large one, painstakingly put together over many months, but it was on just one that the Attorney General, Sir Reginald Manningham-Buller, decided to prosecute Adams. Eighty-one-year-old Mrs Edith Morrell had died in 1950 and the Yard's investigations indicated she had been receiving massive doses of drugs, mainly injections of morphine. She had been a capricious will-maker but at the end had left Adams her Rolls Royce, an oak chest containing a silver service an an Elizabethan cupboard he had always expressed a desire to own. He looked stunned when formally charged with her murder by Hannam. 'Murder?' he asked. 'I do not think you could prove it was murder – she was dying in any event.'

Since 'the Eastbourne Job' had begun, the newspapers of the world had been having a field day, one old lady dozing in a deckchair on the prom being startled awake by a cameraman taking her picture, which appeared in a German newspaper the following day with the caption: 'Is this the one who escaped?' Now the journalists packed the oaken Number One Court at the Old Bailey to watch the Attorney General himself, Manningham-Buller, QC, by tradition prosecuting in a capital murder charge involving poisoning, joust with Mr Geoffrey Lawrence, QC, for the life of Adams. He pleaded 'not guilty' before the judge, Sir Patrick (later Lord) Devlin, and a trial lasting 17 days was under way. Adams was not called upon to utter a word during that time, sitting attentive in the dock every day, sometimes clutching at the rail with white-knuckled hands.

Manningham Buller (nicknamed Bullying Manner because of his approach to defendants when in full stride) was supported in the prosecution by a formidable array of witnesses, the three nurses who had cared for Mrs Morrell, and experts in the world of medicine. But Lawrence conducted a brilliant defence, staggering the Crown early in the trial by producing the nurses' long forgotten medical records, written in flimsy school exercise books.

One phrase in the judge's summing-up was illuminating: 'A man, who on the known facts, was guilty of folly and perhaps worse, might never in his own mind have thought of murder.'

It took the jury of ten men and two women only forty-five minutes to return with a 'not guilty' verdict. Dr Adams, looking flushed, bowed stiffly to the judge. He was later fined £2,400 at Lewes Assizes for forging prescriptions, failing to keep a proper register of dangerous drugs and obstructing the police . . . small beer when you have escaped the noose!

He was also struck off the medical register but was reinstated four years later and continued to practise in genteel Eastbourne until his death in July 1983. He is well remembered in the town in later days for his remarkable cures for hangovers among the guests and staff at one of the big seafront hotels, and for the ex-Hullett Silver Dawn Rolls Royce he lent every year to the Eastbourne Carnival Committee for transporting the Carnival Queen around the town.

John Bodkin Adams was not held in any great esteem as a doctor by his colleagues. Were the patients who encountered the sharp end of his needle at the mercy of a muddled practitioner who used heroin out of mercy . . . or a calculating and avaricious criminal who preyed on the old and helpless? There will always be doubts. As the doctor himself told police during their investigation: 'Easing the passing of a dying person is not all that wicked. She wanted to die – that cannot be murder. It is impossible to accuse a doctor.'

10

LOVERS BY THE SEA

He was the 'Uncrowned King' of Ireland, one of the most powerful leaders in the history of British politics. She was another man's wife. It was a fateful combination that by the values of the last century was to cause a far bigger political scandal than John Profumo, Lord Lambton, Jeffrey Archer or Cecil Parkinson of more recent years.

Charles Stewart Parnell, the Irish Home Rule campaigner, had a passionate affair with Kitty O'Shea, the diminutive daughter of an Essex clergyman, which outraged polite Victorian society and virtually ended hopes of self-government for the Emerald Isle. He was branded a scoundrel and a cad, she was called a scarlet woman and a harlot, but the couple also found a certain amount of sympathy in some quarters to earn the affectionate label of 'lovers by the sea'. They are fondly remembered in Hove where their love blossomed and a plaque commemorating their romance was unveiled in 1986 at Walsingham Terrace, now Dorset Court, where they once shared a house.

Parnell was at the height of his career in the 1880s when he met Kitty at a political dinner party. Ironically, the introduction was made by her husband, Captain William O'Shea, the MP for County Clare. They met again weeks later when Kitty went to see him at the Palace of Westminster. A rose fell from her bosom and the dashing politician picked it up and pressed it to his

45

lips. Before the year was out they had become lovers, escaping together to Brighton and other South Coast hideaways, for discretion was always paramount. Parnell went to enormous lengths to keep the affair a secret, using false names like 'Mr Smith' and 'Mr Fox' to avoid recognition, and on one occasion even shaving off his magnificent beard on the way down on the Brighton train. Not all their time was spent canoodling. They both enjoyed exploring the old streets of Brighton together and Parnell was fascinated by the railway station roof, making many carefully measured drawings of the building.

But their cherished romance was doomed. While he was being entertained by Kitty at her home at 8 Medina Terrace, Hove, they were startled by a loud knock at the front door – Captain O'Shea was outside. Parnell (alias Mr Stewart) had to beat a hasty retreat, so the story goes, via the fire escape.

A close call. There was no escaping the suspicions of the Captain, however, and on Christmas Eve 1889 he filed a petition for divorce naming Parnell, the darling of Ireland, as co-respondent. The politician entered no defence. It was a tremendous opportunity for the Press to let themselves go with lurid pronouncements. Parnell became the most 'infamous adulterer of the century', and Kitty 'a proved British prostitute' and the 'werewolf woman of Irish politics'.

Housekeeper Mrs Caroline Pethers provided the crucial evidence that related to the comings and goings at Medina Terrace. She told the court how one afternoon she went up to the drawing room to light the gas and found her mistress and Mr Parnell behind locked doors. Then the bell rang downstairs – it was Captain O'Shea again. Parnell made himself scarce and ten minutes later rang the same bell and asked for Mrs O'Shea. Mrs Pethers had not seen him go down by the stairs and the suggestion was made that he had got away via the balcony and a fire escape. The housekeeper stated that such incidents had occurred 'two or three times'. There was no cross-examination of the evidence; it could have been torn to shreds if there had been because there was no fire escape at Medina Terrace.

The divorce went through. It was the ruin of Parnell's political career and he was eventually forced to quit the leadership of the Irish Nationalist Party. It did mean, however, that he and Kitty were able to get married and the ceremony duly took place at a register office in Steyning on June 23rd, 1891. A church wedding was, of course, out of the question.

The couple settled at Walsingham Terrace, but their happiness was short-lived. Parnell was suffering acute rheumatic pains and collapsed and died on October 6th. That same rose which he had once pressed ardently to his lips was placed by Kitty in his coffin.

11

NATIONAL LAUGHING STOCK

Picture a vast expanse of open countryside rolling gently down to a majestic coastline of white cliffs. Great green acres with here and there a patch of gorse and trees, an isolated farmhouse or two, a shepherd tending his flock and squinting into the sun as he takes in the panorama of land and sea.

This idyllic rural scene existed in Sussex before the First World War but has now been lost forever. Charles Neville, the big daddy of all land speculators, bought the entire coastal strip from Newhaven to Rottingdean, a distance of some seven miles, from the Marquess of Abergavenny. The price he paid in 1914 was £15,000. Since then the land has been the subject of scandal, controversy and despair.

Few towns have suffered as much abuse as Peace-haven. One critic called it a blot on the landscape. The writer Richard Wyndham went further in *South Eastern Survey*, calling it 'probably the nastiest mess in the British Isles'. Strong stuff. The poor place's very history stems from undesirable circumstances, the 'illegitimate child' of land dealer Neville. He had just returned from Canada when he made his shrewd and momentous purchase, and in North America had been greatly impressed by the Garden City type of development. He resolved to introduce it to the South Coast.

Neville split the land up into plots, 25 ft by 100 ft, and

offered them as prizes in a nationwide competition in 1916 to guess a name for the new resort. The competition appeared in all the national newspapers of the day and generated 80,000 entries. Two people shared the £100 first prize for suggesting the name New Anzac-on-Sea, but 2,445 other people 'won' building plots and were asked to pay a £4 conveyancing fee for the deeds.

The enterprise netted Neville a handsome profit but landed him in trouble with the law. It was declared 'a clever fraud' by the court and he was ordered to pay back the conveyancing fees. The confusion over exactly who did own various patches of land was to persist for more than half-a-century and was the cause of the sporadic development that was the despair of planning experts.

Some prize winners who expected to find an attractive resort well connected by public transport and with an elegant promenade were so disgusted at the reality of the situation that they just wrote the whole thing off to experience. They would have found a muddy wasteland of wooden shacks and tents, no proper roads, few shops and animals grazing among the sparse settlement. No wonder winners were disillusioned: it must have been a great deal worse than a frontier town in the Wild West.

Neville was undaunted by the shocked reactions, however, and forged ahead with his dream of creating homes 'fit for heroes to live in' in the aftermath of the First World War (he is also remembered as the composer of that hymn of the trenches, *Pack Up Your Troubles in Your Old Kit Bag*). Between the wars his resort, now named Peacehaven (New Anzac-on-Sea was a bit of a mouthful), took haphazard shape. The piecemeal building of bungalows on claimed plots prompted one town planning critic to describe it as 'a national laughing stock' and a 'disgusting blot on the landscape'.

This was, of course, in the days before town planning legislation and line upon line of roads stretched out unchecked in a grid system from the one main road that connects Peacehaven with the outside world. Their strange names, Gladys Avenue, Edith Avenue, Phyllis Avenue and the like, are believed to have derived from the wives and girlfriends of the builders. The first influx of inhabitants was accompanied by gigantic loads of building material and an army of a workforce, 1,000 strong. Peacehaven had its own electricity company, water supply, nurseries and even a two-man police force.

Neville was a master of publicity and sent guidebooks to prospective buyers crammed with fanciful artists' impressions of how he hoped his 'Garden City By The Sea' would look. Train loads of potential new settlers were conveyed by chartered buses to the site. Plots of land could be bought for as little as £50 with a down payment of £5. He even splashed out £1,000 to a Dutch pilot to give the country's first powerless gliding display at Peacehaven to put the place well and truly on the map, and made up a song urging people to come and settle.

Lord Teynham was allotted a laborious task in 1925 at a celebration to mark the fifth anniversary of the birth of Peacehaven, when a free house and land were offered in a draw. A total of 766 tickets had been issued to those eligible who could produce a certificate of land ownership, and the noble lord had to draw 300 out of the hat before the winner emerged since all were blanks except one. It was advertised that five more homes would be given away, but there is only a record of one ever having been so.

So the new town sprawled across the clifftops with its satellites Telscombe Cliffs and Saltdean, but if it was an ugly duckling then it is now a swan in the eyes of the people who live there today. East Sussex County Council conducted a series of meetings to try and improve the image of the place and the message that came across was that the locals liked Peacehaven just the way it was. Fiercely proud of the community spirit that had been forged in the space of fifty years and sensitive to adverse criticism, they pointed to the scores of amenity groups and the active social life enjoyed by residents. Nevertheless, in 1973 the county council made a compulsory purchase order for land to be developed as a proper town centre, a new 'heart' of shops and community facilities to give an ever-expanding town a bright future.

Neville certainly foresaw the expansion in his dream of a seaside utopia that became a nightmare. Or maybe he was just touting for business when he prophesied: 'The day will come when there will not be sufficient room for all the people who will desire to come and live with us and I want you to make sure, doubly sure, by coming early. Now, my friends, dividends will be earned and paid if you will follow my advice, the best and finest dividends in the world, for they will be paid in good health, long life, and I hope a happy and contented old age.'

12
THE VANISHING EARL

At around 11.30 p.m. on the night of Thursday, November 7th, 1974, a dark blue Ford Corsair travelled at speed into Uckfield, turned into Church Road and came to an abrupt halt on the gravel driveway of the country house that stood below the spire of Holy Cross Church. A man, distinguished but dishevelled, with a bloodstain on his trousers, climbed out into the stormy night and made his way to the front door. He was admitted and stayed until 1.15 a.m. when he walked back to the car, started the engine and drove away into the night. He has never been seen again.

The disappearance of Richard John Bingham, Seventh Earl of Lucan, was one of the most baffling mysteries of recent years and one which captured the imagination of the public on an international scale. It hads all the ingredients to do so: the haughty peer, a tragic murder, personalities from the exclusive world of the aristocracy and a vanishing act that beat all the resources of the police. At one time it seemed as though everyone in Britain and beyond was on the lookout for Lord Lucan.

The earlier events of that November night were grim. 'Lucky' Lucan was a compulsive gambler in the fashionable clubs of London's West End, staking and often losing thousands of pounds in an evening on the tables. He had separated from his wife Veronica and lost an expensive High Court custody action for their three children. The man with the impeccable background of an inherited title, an Eton education, and officer in the Coldstream Guards was in deep financial trouble. He owed some £34,000 to banks and individuals, had a gambling debt of £10,000 at the Clermont Club, was paying the £2,400 a year rent on his flat in Elizabeth Street, all the bills on his wife's home in Lower Belgrave Street and was giving her £40 a week. On top of that the High Court instructed him to pay the cost of a nanny.

Perhaps he saw the death of his wife as a way out of his problems. Detective Chief Superintendent Roy Ranson pieced together what he believed happened. He said: 'Lucan let himself into the house in Lower Belgrave Street when he thought the nanny Sandra Rivett would be out on her evening off. He waited in the basement kitchen for his wife to come down to make her nine o'clock pot of tea. He took the bulb out of the light socket. When a woman came down into the darkness he thought it was his wife. Sandra and Lady Lucan were similar in size.'

Detective Chief Superintendent Ranson believes Lucan killed the woman with a length of lead piping and bundled her body into a canvas sack. Seconds later as he was washing the blood from his hands he heard with horror the voice of his wife – and realised he had killed the wrong woman. He then tried to kill Veronica but in his confused state allowed her to talk him out of it, and she escaped to a local pub and raised the alarm. Lucan fled in the Ford Corsair he had borrowed from a friend. He stopped to phone his mother the Dowager Countess and told her he had found an intruder at his wife's home and that both she and the nanny were hurt.

Wearing only a pair of grey slacks and a brown polo-neck sweater he made his way to Uckfield and the mansion home of his friends, Ian and Susan Maxwell Scott. Grant's Hill House was all Gothic splendour, set in beautiful grounds with tennis courts and a swimming pool. It was bought by Mr Maxwell Scott's winnings as a professional gambler: on one day alone in 1966 he won £42,000 on the horses which at that time was Ladbrokes' biggest ever payout. He had made several more thousands when his wife gave birth to twins, which he had insured against.

When Lucan arrived that night, Mr Maxwell Scott was staying in London overnight. His wife let Lucan in. He asked for a drink and told her the story he was later to relate in a letter written at Grant's Hill House to his brother-in-law Bill Shand Kydd. Posted in Uckfield the day after the murder it was smeared slightly with blood and described his interruption of an intruder's attack on his wife at Lower Belgrave Street and his fears that his wife would blame him. There was also touching concern for the welfare of his children, whom he adored.

Susan Maxwell Scott, a trained barrister, tried to persuade Lucan to stay the night, but he refused and left her with the impression he was going back to London to 'sort things out'. Before he departed she gave him four Valium tablets.

She had given police their first clues to Lucan's movements on the night of the murder but incurred their wrath by failing to contact them. Mrs Maxwell Scott was only interviewed after the arrival of the Shand Kydd letter and only then did she reveal the type of car Lucan had been driving. The Ford Corsair was discovered abandoned three days after the murder in Norman Road, Newhaven. There were bloodstains on the driver's seat and steering wheel – a mixture of Sandra Rivett's and Lady Lucan's blood groups – and in the boot was a piece of lead piping almost identical to the murder weapon found at the scene.

There were various possibilities of what had happened to the missing Earl. Did he catch the ferry *Senlac* to Dieppe using a 60-hour passport? Did one of his many wealthy friends provide him with a helicopter, small plane or boat at short notice to get him out of the country? Was the car abandoned in Newhaven as a ruse to put the police off his scent? Or, panic-stricken and depressed, did he crawl into the undergrowth on the Sussex Downs and die?

There was a massive police search of the area and amazingly bodies were found, including one of a man who had been missing since 1965. But not Lucan.

Detective Chief Superintendent Ranson believed the Earl was one of the old school who would take the only course of a gentleman caught in a nasty corner. He believed he caught the ferry and committed suicide by throwing himself into the Channel between Newhaven and Dieppe. He also put forward the gruesome theory that if the body had ended up in a fisherman's net it might have been deliberately weighed down or the stomach pierced with a boat hook to send it to the bottom as by law, if the body was brought in by the fisherman his whole catch would be declared contaminated and have to be destroyed.

Over the years thousands of people in Britain have claimed to have seen Lucan, and there were other 'sightings' abroad: in Rhodesia, Poland, Sri Lanka, Australia and practically every Western European country. Every time police have followed up and drawn a blank. Whether is is alive or dead, there was certainly one victim that November night, nanny Sandra Rivett. The verdict at her inquest was: 'Murder by Lord Lucan.'

Like the Earl, Grant's Hill House has disappeared, demolished by Wealden District Council to make way for old people's flats. For those who collect trivial information, there is a suitable if tenuous twist. Lord Lucan's ancestor commanded the cavalry in the Crimean War (1854–1856) and relayed the blundered order that sent the Light Brigade charging to destruction. Leading the far more successful charge of the Heavy Brigade that day was General James Scarlett – who came from Uckfield.

13

BATTLE TO THE DEATH

Cruelty to animals rarely fails to raise the hackles in this nation of animal lovers. So there was widespread horror in Sussex when it was revealed that badger baiting, a savage blood sport outlawed in 1911, had been revived in the county.

Horror became revulsion in the summer of 1984 when details emerged of the 'sport' which had existed in England since the Dark Ages and changed little over a thousand years. A badger and dogs were thrown together into a pit and expected to fight to the death. Traditionally, the English used terriers which, out of blind obedience to man, were trained to attack their fierce opponent at close quarters in the confined space. To give the terriers a better chance the lower jaw of the badger was sometimes broken.

The sheer courage of the badger was supposed to provide the entertainment at these contests, which took place in the dead of night in remote woods. Spectators gathered around the makeshift arena to gamble on the result, torchlight and hurricane lamps throwing monstrous, flickering shadows against the surrounding trees.

The return of an activity considered too unpleasant to remain legal in the less conservation-conscious years before the First World War was brought to light by a Sussex University biology lecturer. Dr Tim Roper had been carrying out research into the social behaviour of badgers in the Ouse valley when he came upon a series of pits between Lewes and Newhaven. One of them, five feet deep and four feet wide with vertical sides, was in the middle of a group of setts, and there was evidence to suggest that the badger had been dug out of his home.

Dr Roper told the Press: 'Besides being illegal, badger baiting is a repulsive activity involving great cruelty both to badgers and to the dogs pitted against them. For the dogs there is at best the chance of escaping with ears torn and muzzles bitten. For the badgers there is the certainty of eventual death through injury and exhaustion'.

They were essentially timid creatures, said Dr Roper, but when cornered became formidable opponents. He was particularly disturbed to find that what was essentially an illicit rural practice confined to the north of the country had spread to the south.

The police confessed that the very nature of badger baiting made it difficult to catch and prosecute offenders. People were urged to be on the alert in the countryside for groups of men near a sett with dogs and spades, and a local farm secretary came forward to say that a furtive bunch fitting this description had been seen in the area and warned that they were trespassing.

Maybe the disturbing story prompted extra vigilance, for there were no more pits found and the bloody contests disappeared as swiftly as they had begun, but it remained a bad year for poor old brock.

Badgers were implicated in the transmission of tuberculosis to cattle after an outbreak of the disease in the downland hamlet of Folkington. The men from the Ministry of Agriculture, Fisheries and Food moved in for a Government sanctioned extermination of the local badger population. They used traps because gassing was shown to be inhumane, and also so live badgers could be tested for research purposes. Some forty-seven badgers were collected (eleven were infected) before furious animal lovers moved in and prevented further trapping from taking place.

The Folkington Badger Action Group mounted a constant watch over a period of two years, living in a small shanty settlement that grew on land provided by a local owner. The Ministry pulled out when they arrived, but the group pledged to remain while the threat existed and maintained a daily check on the setts. When MAFF officials returned briefly they found their every move followed by a large crowd of protesters. It remained the only place in East Sussex where badger control was Ministry policy. It was suspended from May, 1984, when the action group moved in but the situation remained 'under review'.

So the stalemate continued. An irony in Folkington, of all places, for in the 1960s the village played its part in getting a better deal for badgers. Lady Monckton, with the help of her cousin Lord Arran, introduced the Badger Protection Act in the House of Lords.

The case of the action group, on guard in all weathers, was simple. They did not accept that the animals were responsible for cattle infection. They said evidence from other countries suggested the badgers were innocent and asked why the MAFF had not developed a badger vaccine that would end the problem once and for all. On the other side of the coin the Ministry stated there was strong geographical correlation between TB disease outbreaks in badgers and cattle. After thorough research no other apparent source of infection had been found. The farmer's position was also clear. Cattle infected by TB were slaughtered and the farmer not fully compensated for his loss or for the restrictions imposed on his stock as a result of the outbreak.

If the MAFF was not seen to take firm measures against the alleged culprits, then the temptation to farmers to take illegal action was evident. One farmer spelled out his case against the burrowing cousin of the bear amidst the outrage over their persecution: 'We would like those who will see no evil, hear no evil or speak no evil of badgers to know that we are not uncaring, cruel badger-bashers. We have lived with badgers for a very long time . . . but we will not live with tubercular badgers. Infected social groups have to be eliminated quickly.'

The action group involved about forty local people who came in to patrol the area with visitors from throughout the south arriving periodically to offer their support. As the organisers said, it had become more than a badger watch, it had become a focus for people interested in conservation. Their two-year vigil ended in victory when Whitehall stepped in to end the threat to the badgers. A report, Badgers and Bovine TB, confirmed that the slaughter of the animals to control the disease had been unscientific, inhumane and grossly expensive.

14

PILTDOWN MAN

The clandestine activities at an old gravel pit on a warm June day in 1912 attracted enough local curiosity for the Piltdown police constable to be informed. The bobby later went to the clerk to the magistrates at Uckfield, Mr Charles Dawson, and reported: 'Three toffs, two of them from London, have been digging like mad in the gravel at Barkham and nobody could make out what they were up to.'

Dawson himself had been one of the gentlemen sweating away with picks and shovels, but perhaps because the solicitor and keen amateur archaeologist was on the brink of the sort of momentous discovery he had always dreamed of he did not reveal his involvement. Instead, he said the men were probably merely harmless enthusiasts looking for flints in the area and enlisted the constable's help, explaining where flints might be found on his beat and asking him to report anything he might discover. Digging then continued without interference from the police or nosey rustics until winter flooding brought work to a halt.

The expenditure of all this energy in a remote corner of Sussex had its roots four years earlier when Dawson had visited the gravel pit, which supplied the materials for mending the local roads, and was handed a portion of human cranium of unusual thickness by a workman. It was not until some time later that Dawson discovered a

61

second and larger piece of the skull on one of the rain-washed spoil heaps and soon afterwards a portion of hippopotamus tooth.

This sparked a thorough probe by Dawson and his fellow 'toffs': Professor Arthur Smith Woodward, the industrious and humourless keeper of palaeontology at the British Museum, and Teilhard de Chardin, a young Frenchman soon to be ordained as a priest whose interest in archaeology while studying at Hastings had led to his friendship with Dawson.

Various other big noises from the world of archaeology, geology and anthropology joined them that summer and autumn, during which time further pieces of skull were found plus, most exciting of all, a section of jaw bone. They lifted the veil of secrecy that December when *Nature* reported: 'The fossil human skull and mandible to be described by Mr Charles Dawson and Dr Arthur Smith Woodward as we go to press is the most important discovery of its kind ever made in England. The specimen was found in circumstances which seem to leave no doubt of its geological age . . .' *Nature* also asserted that the only real ancestor of modern man was represented by the remains found in Sussex: '. . . Dr Smith Woodward inclines to the theory that the Neanderthal race was a degenerate offshoot of early man while surviving modern man may have arisen directly from the primitive source of which the Piltdown skull provides the first discovered evidence.'

The *Manchester Guardian* was the first to break the news of the discovery to the public at large with a headline less conservative than *Nature*: 'The earliest man? A skull millions of years old. One of the most important of our time.' Eoanthropus Dawsoni – Dawson's Dawn Man, the 600,000-year-old missing link between man and his ancestors, had arrived.

A reconstruction of the skull was made, and caused great excitement and some confusion particularly as the skull was shaped as in a modern man while the jaw was

Shaded
pieces
indicate
Piltdown
'find'

as in a modern ape. Piltdown became a place of pilgrimage for motor coaches laden with natural history societies; penny postcards of the diggings went on sale; the village pub changed its name from The Lamb Inn to The Piltdown Man. They even scheduled the site as a national monument.

63

But from the outset there were doubts about the authenticity, doubts that grew as the years went by and further discoveries of man's origins were made elsewhere in the world. Four decades after Piltdown Man first surfaced, he was subjected to a stringent series of chemical and mechanical tests. The British Museum's report of the investigation, issued in 1953, was damning. It stated that the jaw belonged to a modern ape, the teeth had been deliberately worn down, that fluorine tests revealed most of the skull fragments to be modern, that the black coating on the bones (described by Dawson as 'ferruginous', or iron stain) was in fact a paint-like substance and the coating on the mandible was superficial to make it resemble the cranium. All an unscrupulous and skilful hoax.

But who was the culprit in this forgery that fooled the experts for so long, that brought a motion in the House of Commons on November 25th, 1953, 'That this house has no confidence in the Trustees of the British Museum because of the tardiness of their discovery that the skull of the Piltdown Man is a fake.'

Was it the jovial Dawson, who had died at his Lewes home in 1916 at the age of 62? He was the prime suspect, of course, on the grounds of increasing his own fame, but he was not skilled enough and would have risked early exposure and ignominy.

Ronald Millar, in his book *The Piltdown Men*, points the finger of guilt at the Australian-born Sir Grafton Elliot Smith, an accomplished human anatomist and expert on prehistoric and ancient human skulls, who would have loved a chuckle at the expense of stick-in-the-mud palaeontology and anatomy. Did he slip down to Sussex and plant bits and pieces for the gullible enthusiasts to seize from the dirt with such delight? Perhaps it was an elaborate prank that got out of hand.

In 1978 *Nature* published an account of a tape recording made before his death that year by Professor James Douglas. According to him, the hoax was perpetrated by his former colleague Professor William Johnson Sollas, who worked at Oxford University from 1897 until his death at the age of 87. The hoax was aimed at Sir Arthur Smith Woodward with whom he was having 'a bitter feud'.

An old blacksmith's story of the truth behind Piltdown may be an insult to science but is worth recording as a postscript to a whole episode that was an insult to science. A transcript of the statement made in 1953 by Albert Dudeney was published by the Sussex Archaeological Society in 1980. He claimed that the skull which had foxed everyone may have belonged to a deformed villager from Newick, near neighbour of Piltdown.

Dudeney's mother worked as a maid at Newick's Bull Inn where she became friendly with the ostler, a man 'who was afflicted. He was much more monkey than man, but very intelligent – he had a face like a monkey, his arms were long and thin and he walked with an animal gait.' One afternoon the ostler invited the young maid to visit his cottage. He pulled aside a blind 'and there was a monkey as big as a man chained to the wall'. The ostler said it was his brother, that he could not talk and that only his mother could manage him. Soon afterwards this unhappy creature died. When the maid asked what had happened to the body, the ostler replied: 'It's a secret. I mustn't tell you. You see, you can't bury a monster in hallowed ground because a monster has no soul.'

It later transpired that in years gone by they used to bury horses at Piltdown – 'an appropriate place to bury a monster'. Old Albert Dudeney had put two and two together. He might have made five, but his final theory is as good as any on the whole enigma of Dawn Man: 'If that monkey had been born in the wilds it would be all animal, but as it was born of a woman there would be a certain amount of human in it and that might put the scientists off the track.'

15

FORBIDDEN LOVE

When James Bellingham stepped smartly across the lobby of the House of Commons and pulled out a pistol, he was about to go into the history books (and the Trivial Pursuit box) and to end a tender love affair that had been the talk of 18th century Sussex.

Bellingham shot dead Spencer Perceval to become the only man who has assassinated a British Prime Minister. It ended the meteoric rise of Perceval and the hearts of an enraged nation went out to his distraught widow. In her sorrow, her mind must have gone back to happier days when a forbidden love blossomed.

She was the beautiful daughter of Sir Thomas Spencer Wilson, of Searles, Fletching, a respected member of the county's landed gentry. Her eldest sister had married the Honourable Charles Perceval so it was natural that she should form a friendship with the bridegroom's brother Spencer, second son of the Earl of Egmont. Friendship became a love affair, but it was a relationship that looked doomed. Sir Thomas had seen Charles, the heir to a title, as a highly suitable match, but young Spencer, with no expectations and at that time a briefless barrister, was a different proposition and the affair was frowned upon and then actively discouraged.

When Jane came of age she went to East Grinstead on a visit to stay with Thomas Wakeham, an attorney who lived at The Hermitage and was also estate agent at

Searles for the Wilson family. Spencer met her there and, whether by design or on impulse, they were married at East Grinstead on August 10th, 1790.

The fact that the bride wore her riding habit at the ceremony suggests it was a spur of the moment decision. The wedding took place 'amid the ruins of the parish church', the building being wrecked when the tower collapsed and repairs still being under way. But one of Perceval's relatives, writing to a friend about the event nearly a century later, maintained that the ceremony was conducted in a blacksmith's shed. The parish register contains the entry: '1790. Hon Spencer Perceval of Lincolns Inn, bachelor, to Jane Wilson, spinster of this parish, married by licence 10th August 1790 by me, Charles Whitehead, vicar.' The witnesses were the attorney friend Thomas Wakeham and his wife Dorothy.

Jane's father was, of course, conspicuous by his absence, and what amounted to an elopement was the gossip of Sussex dinner tables and servants' quarters for weeks. Later Sir Thomas Wilson let it be known that he had decided to give way to the romance in view of his daughter's continuing affection for Spencer, but felt he could not do so publicly. He had therefore discreetly remained ignorant but sent his daughter to Thomas Wakeham so the matter could be arranged. Perhaps this was the story he put about after Spencer became a successful and wealthy politician.

Certainly the marriage was a happy and fruitful one despite its inauspicious start (the couple had 12 children) and Spencer's career developed rapidly. In 1796 he became King's Counsel and later that year, when his sixth child was born, he was returned to Parliament unopposed when a vacancy arose in Northampton. He became Solicitor General, in 1802 Attorney General and in that capacity prosecuted one Colonel Despard for high treason. In 1807 he was appointed Chancellor of the Exchequer under Portland and succeeded him as Prime Minister in 1809.

67

Three years later he met his end at the hands of John Bellingham, not a political opponent but a bankrupt with a personal grievance against the Government. Bellingham, described as 'a man of disordered brain', saw the origin of his grudge in the refusal of the English ambassador at St Petersburg to interfere with the regular process of Russian law under which he had been arrested. Bellingham applied to Perceval for redress and the inevitable refusal inflamed his crazy resentment.

On Monday, May 11th 1812, as Perceval was passing through the lobby of the House of Commons, Bellingham placed a pistol to his breast and fired. The Prime Minister died before a doctor could be found. He was buried on May 16th in Lord Egmont's family vault at Charlton. Bellingham was tried at the Old Bailey on May 15th where his plea of insanity was set aside by the court. He was hanged on May 18th, one week after the assassination.

And the mourning Jane? Two days after Spencer's death Parliament voted a pension of £2,000 a year to Mrs Perceval and a sum of £50,000 to be invested for the benefit of her large family.

16

THE GREAT BEAST

He called himself 'The Great Beast' and the newspapers called him 'The Wickedest Man in the World'. He inspired international condemnation as a master of the occult and slavish devotion among his followers. He was at once an unscrupulous tyrant and an enigmatic genius.

But the majority of people in Hastings never suspected the awesome reputation and colourful past of the thin old gentleman who lived in a boarding house. With his pipe and tweeds he looked like any retired colonel. Certainly the top brass at Hastings Chess Club, of which he was a keen member and to which he presented a handsome chess set, would have thought twice about renewing his subscription if they had known he was a heroin addict who sometimes took as much as eleven grains a day (the normal dose would be one-eighth of a grain).

Aleister Crowley's lifetime of controversy was drawing to a rather pathetic close in the seaside town. But he still had one more major scandal to cause.

He was born Edward Alexander Crowley in 1875, the son of a wealthy brewer who had retired to Leamington to devote his life to the doctrines of the Plymouth Brethren. In Crowley's autobiography he made it clear that much of his later 'diabolism' was a revolt against his strict religious upbringing. He went to public school in Malvern and then on to Oxford where he acquired a passion for rock climbing and published his own poems.

69

He also produced a sadistic, pornographic short novel called *Snowdrops from a Curate's Garden.*

Crowley, a student of chemistry, was introduced to an 'alchemist' called George Cecil Jones and through him to the order of the Golden Dawn, a magical group that left him disappointed in the mediocrity of its members and ceremonies. Magic was an instinct for him rather than an intellectual impulse, and he saw it as the key to unlocking the powers of his own will.

He took a flat in London and started calling himself Count Vladimir Svareff and cultivated a Russian accent. When he moved to a house beside Loch Ness he adopted a kilt and called himself the Laird of Boleskin. While in Scotland he concentrated on the magic of Abra-Melin the Mage, with the aim of contacting his Guardian Angel. But there were more sinister happenings. Crowley stated that the lodge and terrace of Boleskin House became peopled with shadowy shapes, the lodgekeeper went mad and tried to kill his wife and children, and the room became so gloomy when Crowley tried to copy magic symbols that he needed artificial light, even though the sun blazed outside.

After playing a key role in the dissolution of the Golden Dawn, with which he had a grudge because they refused to allow him to rise in the order's rankings, the Laird left for Mexico where he claimed that concentrated effort almost enabled his own image to disappear in the mirror. He then suffered something of a crisis: whether to continue his magical quest or abandon it and simply develop a power of immense concentration. He settled for the life of the rich playboy, hunting big game in Ceylon, exploring the Irrawaddy River in a canoe and, in 1902, being one of the party that failed through bad weather and illness to climb K2 in India, the second highest mountain in the world.

In Paris he became a notorious figure among the artistic set and was portrayed in *The Magician* by W. Somerset Maugham. Back in Boleskin, he was introduced to

Rose, the unstable widowed sister of a young painter called Gerald Kelly. She had a number of suitors and Crowley said that by marrying him she could be free of them and yet leave their marriage unconsummated. They were married the next morning to the fury of Rose's family and it was a platonic relationship that lasted only a few hours.

Rose was to become a dypsomaniac and later went insane, a pattern that recurred among people who became too intimate with Crowley. It was during their strange relationship that he heard a musical voice from the corner of the room which instructed him to take up his fountain pen and dictated *The Book of the Law* to him, assuring Crowley that it would be translated into many languages. Its fundamental message was: 'Do what thou wilt', and it is plainly Crowley, with the religious hang-over from childhood, who advises: 'Be goodly therefore; dress ye all in fine apparel; eat rich foods and drink sweet wines and wines that foam! Also take your fill and will of love as ye will, when, where and with whom ye will . . .' It was his own Koran and he was the chosen prophet.

He published more poetry, a book praising himself (*The Star in the West* by J. F. C. Fuller who received the £100 prize offered by Crowley for the best essay on his works) and a bi-annual journal of magic called *The Equinox*. He started his own magical society called The Silver Star, knighted himself, shaved his head and divorced his wife. In 1910 he hired Caxton Hall for the performance of a series of rites which 'would induce religious ecstasy' and charged five guineas for admission. They were reviewed with hostility in the Press and from then on it was all downhill: magical ceremonies, mistresses, frantic attempts to raise money, newspaper attacks on him and efforts to justify himself in print.

He entered the world of sex magic with a will with both male and female disciples, including a troop of chorus girls in Moscow called the Ragged Ragtime Girls. Crowley, who had taken to defecating on people's carpets unashamedly, had by now sharpened his two canine teeth to a sharp point and when introduced to women would greet them on the wrist or the neck with 'a serpent's kiss'.

He was in America during the First World War where he adopted the role of the anti-British Irishman (he had never even been to Ireland) and wrote violent anti-British propaganda for a newspaper called *The Fatherland*. Though his fortune had long since run out, he maintained his bizarre lifestyle through the generosity of followers, of whom he was never short.

Leah Hirsig, the nude subject of one of his paintings called *Dead Souls*, became pregnant by him and they rented a farmhouse in Sicily, which he decorated with pornographic pictures and demons, and indulged in sex magic together with the nursemaid Ninette Shumway. Drugs were also a feature of the lifestyle. The strange goings on at the farmhouse reached the British Press when a young disciple died after drinking the blood of a sacrificed cat and his wife exposed the story to *John Bull*. Benito Mussolini did not like the publicity and ordered Crowley and his menage to leave the island. Leah took up with Norman Mudd, a mathematics professor and devotee of Crowley's works who had presented him with his life's savings. Crowley did not seem to mind and defiantly amused himself with a small negro boy before landing on his feet when a rich American woman fell under his spell. Mudd later committed suicide.

Crowley was now a notorious figure and no bookshops dared to stock the first volume of his *Confessions*. He was ordered out of France in 1929, banned from lecturing at Oxford and the owner cancelled the lease of a house in London where he was due to stage an exhibition of his paintings. His latest mistress, Maria Teresa de Miramar, was not allowed to enter Britain so he took the extraordinary step of marrying her. The marriage was soon dissolved and she later went insane, as did a nineteen-year-old German girl for whom Crowley staged a phoney suicide in an effort to get her back after the magic depressed her and she fled for Berlin. One of his last recorded mistresses was of a less submissive nature and during a particularly furious row she stabbed him with a carving knife.

Crowley refused to slip into middle-aged obscurity and in the 1930s sued Soho character Nina Hamnett for referring to him as a black magician in her autobiography, *Laughing Torso*. She had raised the suggestion (only to dismiss it) that a baby had disappeared at the Sicilian farmhouse. When a number of witnesses had described Crowley's magical activities, the judge, Mr Justice Swift stopped the case and said 'he had never heard such dreadful, horrible, blasphemous and abominable stuff as that which has been produced by the man who describes himself . . . as the greatest living poet'. The jury found against him and he was bankrupted.

So he came to Netherwood, the boarding house at The Ridge in Hastings; a bored old man, addicted to alcohol and drugs, who found the lonely evenings frightening and suffered from bronchitis. He died at the age of 72 on December 5th, 1947, but even after his death succeeded in creating an uproar. A shamelessly phallic poem, *Hymn to Pan*, was read aloud at the funeral service. The reaction of the public to Crowley's gleeful farewell was high indignation and angry letters in the newspapers. Brighton Council had to give an assurance that it would take all steps to see that such an incident was never repeated.

17

A BOX OF STONES

Matrimonial discord is a prime ingredient for causing outrage among friends and neighbours. Sussex has had its fair share of husbands and wives who did not kiss and make up, from the wife kept imprisoned for four years in a room at a Mayfield pub to the unfortunate lady at Ninfield who was sold by her husband for half a pint of gin.

But one of the nastiest cases of injustice against a spouse occurred at Graffham, so nasty that it brought a curse upon a house. The history of the downland village had been one of private ownership and it was largely a benevolent autocracy except in early Georgian times, when Garton Orme was the young squire. He was, by tradition, a veritable ogre.

He starved his wife to death for the sake of a village beauty who had taken his fancy. The villagers were sure he flung the emaciated body down a well, but Orme produced a coffin, there was a funeral service and it was interred in the family vault near the altar. There the coffin, and the scandal rested for more than a century. When certain alterations were made at the church in the 1840s the coffin was brought to light again. The rector, the Rev. Henry Manning, was surprised by its unusual weight and he ordered it to be opened. Inside was nothing but stones.

Small wonder that there is a ghost story in Graffham,

of a sad, pale figure of a woman seen standing beside that fatal well, even in modern times.

So village tradition is borne out by fact. But there have been other stories, more fanciful perhaps, built up around the dastardly deed of Squire Orme. He was supposedly suffering heavy losses at the card table (that curse of the Georgian age) which was making his domestic affairs difficult. He knew that tucked away somewhere in the Elizabethan manor house was a horde of golden Spanish doubloons, the Armada spoils of an ancestor which the young squire had not been able to find. They would solve his debts . . . debts which rankled with his wife, who was bitterly opposed to his gambling habits. He in turn had a brooding grievance against her, the fact that she had not borne him any children. Soon after embarking on his affair with a girl in the village he must have started to ponder 'if only my wife was out of the way'.

Orme obviously decided how she could be removed, locking her away from the outside world and from the servants within the house, watching her waste away little by little. No doubt illness was the excuse he offered for her sudden disappearance from society. Did she actually starve to death or did he finish her off with his own hand at the end? For some reason the corpse would have been too shocking to be explained away as death by natural causes, so he used the well. When it was over he probably had to grease a few palms to buy silence about what was really contained in the coffin at the mock funeral.

After a decent length of time had elapsed he made his way back into village life, trying to ignore the whispering about him and the furtive, suspicious glances. It was not to his lover that he turned, but to the rector's youngest daughter and in due course they were married. The lover remained on the scene, however, and became pregnant. The girl's furious father could get no redress at the great house, so under a willow tree one dark night he laid a savage curse on Orme and his descendants, that every successor at the manor house should not pass on the heritage to a male heir. Orme died in 1758, leaving only a single daughter to inherit. Her husband's building works at the manor brought to light the missing doubloons – though he was abroad when they began to circulate – and this couple, too, had only one daughter.

With her death the inheritance passed elsewhere, and so it was with the next four owners, the manorial lands leaving the family concerned, daughters being the heiresses as there were either no sons or no sons who survived their parents. There followed a bishop, Samuel Wilberforce, the famous Victorian preacher who was lord of the manor for 32 years. His son Reginald succeeded him and it was Reginald who sought to exorcise the evil influence by solemnly burning the willow tree under which the curse of vengeance had been made. It did not seem to make much difference and the strange lack of males continued until after the Second World War.

It is a story reminiscent of the curse of Cowdray, barely five miles away from Graffham. The abbot of despoiled Battle Abbey warned that the line of Sir Antony Browne would perish by fire and water. It was a delayed action curse. Some two hundred years passed before Cowdray House went up in flames in 1793 and soon afterwards Viscount Montagu was drowned in the Rhine. His only sister, who inherited, was the mother of two sons both of whom were drowned while bathing at Bognor.

18

HATRED, RIDICULE OR CONTEMPT

Strange to think that a cheque for £5 could cause a brewery to turn sour, put a bank on the road to ruin and exercise some of the best legal brains in the country. But, then, the law of libel is a complex one.

In the language hallowed by centuries of repetition in the courts libel is publication of any statement which exposes a man to 'hatred, ridicule or contempt'.

Hentys were a famous firm of Chichester brewers who also owned a large number of pubs in Sussex and Hampshire to which they supplied their own brew of beer. They allowed their accounts with these pubs to be settled from time to time with cheques which the tenant landlords had cashed across the bar to oblige customers. The brewery paid these cheques into the Chichester branch of the Capital and Counties Bank.

This system ran into trouble in 1878 when a new bank manager arrived at the Chichester branch and refused to cash cheques drawn on other branches of his bank by persons unknown to him. It was a silly decision, provoked by a cheque for just £5 and only two other similar cheques for a total of £42 had been presented during the year. When Hentys threatened to tell their customers not to cash cheques drawn on the bank, the bank manager refused to give way and replied: 'I am quite indifferent as to your sending out orders to your tenants not to cash our cheques.' The brewery took up the challenge, sending 137 of their customers and tenants occupying their pubs a printed notice which said: 'Messrs Henty & Sons hereby give notice that they will not receive in payment cheques drawn on any of the branches of the Capital and Counties Bank.'

Within a month the notice had caused a run of no less than £277,000 on the bank. It issued a writ against Hentys for libel, claiming £20,000 damages, on the grounds that the notice was tantamount to saying that the bank was insolvent or on the verge of insolvency. Hentys denied that the notice had any such meaning, and pleaded that in the circumstances they had a lawful interest in sending their communication to their customers.

The case was tried by Lord Chief Justice Coleridge and a special jury. The bank's argument was, of course, the interpretation placed on the notice by a large number of its customers. Yet the brewery had done something it was entitled to do – refuse the cheques of a particular bank – and there was no other way it could have expressed refusal except by written notice. The bank retorted that there should have been some statement explaining the reason for the notice which would have avoided unfavourable inference and a damaging reflection on the bank's status. The Lord Chief Justice thought the circular might have a defamatory meaning and left the question to the jury. It failed to agree and was discharged – and the case dragged on.

It was finally decided in the House of Lords that the notice could not be defamatory, and the bank lost its action. Perhaps the yokel supping his pint of Hentys in the pub paused to ponder the intracacies of law and reputation as the dust settled on a battle that finally ended four years after it had begun, was considered by four courts and eleven judges, whose pronouncements took up more than seventy closely-printed pages.

19

THE DEADLY CHOCOLATES

Breezy Brighton is still a place synonymous with naughtiness despite attempts at a more up-market image; gaudy as a saucy seaside postcard beneath that splendid Regency facade, deliciously seedy in the streets that lead inland from the well-manicured promenade. A place that has inspired more nudges and winks than any other town in Britain through its reputation for illicit weekends, where the legion Mr and Mrs Smiths in the hotel register books down the years are testaments to liaisons that have been passionate, romantic and downright sordid.

All part of the fun of being beside the seaside, to be treated with a cheerful discretion by chambermaids and late night porters. But a century and more ago a romantic infatuation that became an irrational passion struck real fear into the hearts of the townfolk. Christiana Edmunds was a 42-year-old spinster in 1870, looking after her widowed mother at a house in Gloucester Place. It must have been a lonely and claustrophobic existence for a woman well past the bloom of youth and with only a bleak decline into old age to look forward to. Her elderly mother may well have been a considerable trial for there was a history of insanity in the family.

Christiana was ripe for excitement, preferably of a romantic nature, and she found it while strolling on Brighton seafront. It was here that she received a glance from local physician Dr Beard. It was a glance devastating in its effect for she promptly fell madly in love with him.

She found out his name and where he lived and after having herself formally introduced, continued their acquaintance through the post. She sent him a stream of letters, many of them written entirely in Italian and flowery in style. He was a kindly man and made the mistake of responding to her, though there was never any suggestion that for his part the relationship was anything more than a rather odd friendship. The romance was all in Christiana's mind.

A woman whose experience of men was limited became deeply devoted to this seaside doctor in a way that was naive; a teenage yearning for unrequited love. But there remained a cold and calculatng side to her nature that realised an obstacle stood in the way of her future life of happiness with Dr Beard. The obstacle was called Mrs Beard.

In March 1871 she paid a visit to the doctor's house, exchanged pleasantries with his wife and offered her a chocolate cream. Mrs Beard became violently ill and the doctor, suddenly suspicious and fearful, forbade Miss Edmunds to have anything more to do with him or his family.

The rejection seems to have killed every romantic notion Christiana held and severed her grip on reality. The story of the chocolate with the less than satisfying centre had got about and she threatened the doctor with an action for slander. When this failed to get a response she embarked upon a wild scheme to convince him that she was not a poisoner. On two occasions she sent a child to buy chocolate creams from a sweet shop, injected them with arsenic or strychnine, and despatched another child back to the shop to have them changed for another kind of confectionery. The poisoned chocolates went back in the shop window and the result, inevitably, was tragic. Little Sidney Albert Barker, aged four, died after eating one of the chocolates.

Christiana herself played a vociferous role in the outrage that followed the little boy's death. She accused the
poor sweet shop proprietor of selling contaminated goods
and became something of a local heroine at the dead
child's inquest when she roundly attacked the police for
not apprehending the perpetrator of this vile crime.

Soon afterwards mysterious packages started to arrive
through the post at addresses throughout Brighton. They
contained gifts of cakes, fruit or sweets and were accompanied by letters written in an unfamiliar hand but
apparently by someone who knew the recipient. Many of
those who sampled the goodies became seriously ill.

Brighton became a town gripped by suspicion and
terror. Spurred on by Christiana's continued attacks on
them (she pointed out that she, too, had received one of
the gifts) and her continued demands for action, the
police eventually offered a reward for information on the
mysterious poisoner through the post. A local chemist
recalled he had supplied Christiana with strychnine and
Dr Beard grew thoughtful. Handwriting was compared
with her Italian-style missives to him and it was established that she had forged letters in order to obtain
poison. She was later to say that she needed the poison to
get rid of some troublesome cats.

Christiana was found guilty of the murder of Sidney
Barker and the attempted murder of Mrs Beard. Her plea
of pregnancy proved false and she was condemned to
death. In the event, however, she escaped the noose for a
life infinitely more wretched than the one in prospect for
her before that fateful glance from Dr Beard – she was
committed for life to an asylum and died at Broadmoor at
the age of 78.

20
CONDUCT UNBECOMING

There was a buzz of excitement in Brighton in the summer of 1840. The 11th (Prince Albert's own) Hussars were to be stationed in the town as a guard for the Royal Pavilion, built by Nash for George IV and rumoured to now become a fashionable retreat for Queen Victoria and her Consort. What more fitting troops to garrison the elegant resort than this crack regiment in their gorgeous uniforms of gold and blue with cherry-red trousers? How exciting it would be for the young ladies of the town to be squired by the dashing (and rich) young officers, or to hear the celebrated regimental band play on the Chain Pier, or to watch the spectacular and numerous reviews staged on the Race Hill above the town when the cavalry wheeled, cantered and charged in perfect precision.

Brighton's tip-top society looked forward to an interesting new social life. They did not bargain on being part of one of the greatest court-martial scandals of the 19th century.

For all their magnificence, the 'Cherrybums' were not a happy body of men. There were pronounced jealousies and factions among the officers, brought about by the ferocious and often maniacal discipline of the man who had purchased command of the regiment and rode at its head into the town on that June day: James Thomas Brudenell, Seventh Earl of Cardigan.

This extraordinary aristocrat was portrayed by his

critics as one of the arch-villains of Victorian England. His private life was a public scandal. He was hissed at the theatre, blackballed forty-six times by a leading military club and tried for intent to murder by the House of Lords. He was arrogant, hopelessly vain and belligerent.

He had made his regiment the most elegant in the army, and they settled in swiftly enough with some of the troops at Preston Barracks and others quartered in Church Street, near the pavilion itself, where they were permitted by the Queen to use the royal stables (now the Dome). Cardigan and his aristocratic officers moved into the grandest hotel, the Royal York, where they dined on the best of food and wine. The commander later leased the best available mansion in Brunswick Square, which became the scene of lavish parties for his friends and the local gentry.

He staged a dinner and ball there on the evening of August 25th where the guests included Mrs Cunynghame, one of the Brighton 'fashionables', and her daughter. Mrs Cunynghame innocently asked Lord Cardigan why two young officers, both called Reynolds though not related, were not present. 'I have not invited them,' said Cardigan with gruff displeasure. The lady was intrigued and pressed the point further. His lordship's voice rose above the strains of the band as he delivered his final pronouncement on the Captains Reynolds: 'As long as I live, they shall never enter my house!'

In fact, John Reynolds was in disgrace for bringing a black bottle (of Moselle) to the regimental mess 'which should be conducted like a gentleman's table, and not like a tavern or pot-house'. Richard Anthony Reynolds had done nothing to officially incur his commander's unpredictable displeasure but was a well-known opponent of Cardigan and his undisguised contempt for officers who had served in India, whom he considered to be lax in discipline and probably poor because they could

not afford to exchange to another regiment. When the
conversation at the ball was relayed to Reynolds he saw
the chance of striking a damaging blow against his
hated lieutenant-colonel, and sent the following letter to
Cardigan at his Brunswick Square home:

'My Lord, – A report has reached me that on Tuesday
last, at a large party given by your lordship, when
asked why the Captains Reynolds were not present,
your lordship replied – "As long as I live they shall
never enter my house." I cannot but consider this
report highly objectionable, as it is calculated to convey

85

an impression prejudicial to my character, and I therefore trust your lordship will be good enough to author-
ise me to contradict it. – I am, my lord, your lordship's
obedient servant,

Richard Anthony Reynolds'

Cardigan took Reynolds aside while the 11th Hussars
were on field exercise on the Downs the following day,
telling him he had no reply to his letter which he considered to be of 'an improper nature'. Reynolds attempted
to argue but was bawled down by Cardigan. The young
captain continued to grumble among his comrades, saying he had been insulted. He wanted the satisfaction
which one gentleman owed to another and wrote to
Cardigan the same day demanding it.

> 'Your Lordship's reputation as a professed duellist . . .
> does not admit of your privately offering insult to me,
> and then securing yourself under the cloak of com-
> manding officer; and I must be allowed to tell your
> Lordship, that it would far better become you to select
> a man whose hands are untied for the object of your
> reproaches, or to act as many a more gallant fellow
> than yourself has done, and waive that Rank which
> your Wealth and Earldom alone entitle you to hold.'

The letter was, as the Horse Guards General Order of
October 20th put it, 'calculated to excite' Lord Cardigan.
To refuse a duelling challenge might be the action of a
coward, but to fight Reynolds would be a breach of military law and etiquette. Cardigan had Captain Reynolds
placed under arrest to await a general court martial.

In keeping with Brighton gentility, the terms of the
arrest were simply that he moved out of the Royal York
Hotel, where most of Cardigan's supporters lived, to
Edlin's Gloucester Hotel. The band of the 11th (Prince
Albert's own) Hussars continued to play and the expensive carriages rolled by between the hotels of the con-
tending parties which faced each other across the green

expanse of the Steine, but there was no more talk of a regimental inspection by Victoria and Albert.

Field officers and press reporters converged on the town for the court-martial on September 25th. It was the sensation of the season and a boon to Brighton society and its guests, as the *Sussex Advertiser* remarked: 'The idlers at this place ought to feel obliged to Lord Cardigan and his antagonists for finding them an interesting topic of conversation, while they were constrained to stay indoors during the equinoctial storms that raged the greater part of last week, and to tell the truth the squabbles of his Lordship have been the all-engrossing theme of conversation in every company both public and private that met here during the last ten days.'

The anti-Cardigan press portrayed Reynolds as the romantic paragon of a gallant hussar, whose dark flashing eyes and stalwart frame caused many a female heart to flutter. It was reported that he had received numerous visits from the well-heeled and influential to wish him well at his trial. It took place in a hospital ward at the cavalry barracks, temporarily converted into a courtroom, with an immense crowd of journalists and sightseers pressing into the corridor and round the windows. It was almost like a siege as the proceedings got under way and Reynolds was charged with conduct 'unbecoming an Officer and a Gentleman, prejudicial to the interests of the Service, subversive of Good Order and Military Discipline'. Cardigan, as prosecutor, was 'all but overwhelmed with emotion' when he came to the imputation of cowardice against him in Reynolds' second letter. According to some spectators, he actually wept with rage. The President, Major-General the Honourable Sir Hercules Pakenham, and thirteen other officers, assisted by the Judge Advocate, watched impassively.

Reynolds could hardly deny sending the letters, and attempted to justify his conduct by showing that Cardigan had ruled the regiment by arrogance and insult and had provoked the challenge. The court was adjourned, but the press continued to debate and the Brighton and London papers were daily filled with editorials and letters on the subjects of the Black Bottle scandal and his Lordship's alleged insults to 'Indian Officers'. The President deplored this and mentioned the possibility of banning further reporting. This only increased the fascination of the trial still further.

On October 1st a crowd of quite unexpected size and determination besieged the courtroom, surging down the corridor, tearing the door off its hinges and smashing the glazed panels either side of it. When Reynolds concluded his speech with 'I hope by your verdict of "not guilty" you will prove to Lord Cardigan that wealth and rank do not license him, although the commanding officer of a regiment, to trample with impunity upon honourable men, who have devoted their lives to the service of our country' the room rang with applause and cheering for several minutes.

Cardigan, naturally, denied provoking the anger of his officers and ever having said at his ball that the Captains Reynolds would never enter his house. Mrs Cunynghame, the only person who could confirm or deny this, had conveniently left for the Continent before the court-martial so she would not be called as a witness.

National indignation was given full reign when the findings of the court were announced on October 20th – Reynolds had been in breach of 'The Articles of War' and was sentenced to be cashiered. He became a hero of the anti-Cardigan Radicals, there were penny subscriptions the length of the country and public meetings in support of him, and reports of large and violent demonstrations against his commander.

The papers were filled with letters of support for him from such pseudonymous correspondents as 'An Old Adjutant', 'Not One of the 11th, I Thank God!' or 'A Lover of Justice, a Hater of Tyranny, and an Admirer of the Gallant and Noble Spirit Which Beats in the Bosom of Captain Reynolds'.

The scandal went right to the highest quarters, with Prince Albert declining to become involved with either side in the dispute. It was a crusade against the abuse of military power which ended, to the astonishment of the Radicals, when their mascot Reynolds admitted publicly that he had 'greviously offended' against army regulations by challenging Cardigan to a duel. Though the loss of his commission was bitter to him 'no degree of provocation can ever justify a subordinate in breaking from the strict line of respectful submission'. After two years of 'remaining quiet', he was gazetted a captain in the 9th Lancers in 1842.

The public had not finished with Cardigan, however. When he appeared in a box at the Theatre Royal in Brighton there were hisses and groans and for half-an-hour it was impossible to begin the performance. After sitting impassively in his box throughout the storm of insults, Cardigan at last withdrew to the accompaniment of three cheers for Captain Reynolds and 'three groans for the Earl of Cardigan'. The Brighton Guy Fawkes celebrations on November 5th lacked the traditional guy. In its place a dummy dressed in the uniform of the 11th (Prince Albert's own) Hussars was paraded gleefully through the streets.

Cardigan moved on to fresh regimental rows, public squabbles and national scandals; a man thirsting for military glory that seemed further and further out of reach as the years went by. His destiny lay in twenty unforgettable minutes in a fold in the rugged hills of the Crimean peninsula. Twenty minutes that transformed him in the eyes of the British public from a villain to a hero as he led the Light Brigade in their futile charge to decimation against the Russian guns in 1854. Whatever his other faults, his lordship did not lack physical courage.

21

A FORTUNE TO BEAT THE DEVIL

It was something of an understatement when someone in Newick said it had outstripped the weather as the principal topic of conversation. The fact that a self-confessed Satanist conned wealthy Sussex Christians out of a fortune had made the sleepy village the focus of international attention.

Derry Mainwaring Knight, said to have been dedicated at birth to the Devil by his grandmother and baptised in human blood, took his place in the dock for a trial which lasted more than two months, which cost around £1 million and which was dubbed one of the most bizarre of the century. It was the fortune spent to beat the Devil; the 'Satan Sting' trial.

Knight was accused of conning his way to more than £200,000 by claiming he could use the money to destroy a Satanic organisation, an order he said he wanted to be free from but which had deep holds on him and to which he had taken vows. If two large debts were to be repaid, the former painter and decorator suggested, he could be freed. He also needed funds to purchase articles of Satanic regalia and instruments which could then be destroyed forever. About £216,000 was paid to Knight between February 1984 and May 1985 by wealthy Christians in the county. He frittered it away, the prosecution said, on rich living, prostitutes and exotic motor cars. He was the man who invariably walked around with a wad of £50 notes in his pocket.

The Rev. John Baker, the rector of Newick, was the man who collected the vast sums of money in his crusade to win Knight's deliverance from evil. The cash came from the committed faithful including Mrs Susan Sainsbury, wife of Hove MP Tim Sainsbury; Viscount Brentford of Newick Park; Michael Warren, a Sussex magistrate; Viscount Hampden, of Glynde Place; and the Earl of March, owner of Goodwood Racecourse.

Mr Baker described an evening when he was praying with Knight, who stayed at the Rectory for several months, and sought to discover the grounds for the demonic activity in his life. A voice speaking from the mouth of Knight had said: 'You cannot have him. He belongs to Lucifer. He was dedicated by sacrifice as a child and he is a Master of the Occult.' When asked at the trial if he thought Knight's trances were an act, the rector replied: 'If they were he should be set free immediately and put in charge of the National Theatre.'

Over the nine weeks at Maidstone Crown Court, the jury heard of the ruthless nature of the Satanists who would kill those who revealed their secrets, of Knight's passion for expensive cars and eye for pretty young girls, of his boast that he had never come across a person he could not part from their money, of his involvement with drugs and prostitution, and of an order to him by Satanists to terminate the trial by pleading guilty. He had resisted that command, he said.

He was found guilty on 19 charges of obtaining cash and property by deception and in jailing him for seven years and fining him £50,000 Judge Neil Dennison said: 'You have been convicted, on evidence that for my part I find compelling, of a clever, calculated and above all callous fraud.' Knight, looking more like a respectable stockbroker with his spectacles and receding grey hair than like the sinister character some imaginations may have conjured from the nature of the case, merely said 'thank you' as he was led away.

Prayers were said for the prisoner in the 11th century parish church in Newick the following Sunday and so the dust settled in the community which had been featured almost daily for two months alongside Devil worship, the black arts and the occult in the newspapers and on television. No wonder the state of the weather took a back seat. Villagers held mixed views on the scandal: Some felt the rector, though sincere in what he had tried to achieve, had brought about a loss of credibility both in himself and in the church. Others maintained he was trying to save a soul and that those who criticised him were confusing Christianity with respectability. He was a caring rector who had acted with courage.

Mr Baker, a member of the International Brotherhood of Magicians and keen conjuror in his spare time under the stage name Presto John, said that throughout the case he was at all times in submission to his superiors. He had consulted five bishops, 12 ministers and at least five lay experts. At no time whatever had his personal integrity been called into question by anyone.

He answered a national Press claim that Satanism was rife in Sussex with the assurance that it certainly did not exist in Newick, but had a warning on the dangers people faced by getting involved with the occult, particularly the black arts. He said: 'I believe there are a lot of people in the black arts who are held in it by fear and who would like to get out. The only way is through Jesus Christ . . . and a minister who understands this realm and can keep his mouth shut.'

22

THE ONION PIE MURDER

Love may be a many-splendoured thing, but it can also cause a whole heap of trouble. Rarely, though, does it lead to the sort of tragedy that destroyed a village's peaceful dignity and led to a young woman's death in front of a baying mob.

Chiddingly is still haunted by the memory, and possibly the ghost, of Sarah Ann French who poisoned her husband with an onion pie so she could marry the man she really loved. She was hanged at Lewes in 1852, the last woman in Sussex to pay the ultimate penalty as a spectacle for the public, and is still believed to haunt an old house near The Six Bells at Chiddingly.

It was at The Six Bells that rumours spread that Sarah French had poisoned her husband. He was a farm labourer at nearby Sheen Farm. On Christmas Eve in 1851 he had complained of stomach pains and by early January he was dead.

The local coroner had already recorded a verdict of 'death from natural causes' but such was the gossip that the body of French was exhumed and placed in the belfry at Chiddingly church. A fresh jury met at the pub and unravelled a sordid tale. It came out that Sarah French was in love with the young suitor of her sister. She had told him she would marry him if she was free, and it was discovered that she had bought arsenic not long before

her husband's death. With that evidence the jury returned a verdict of wilful murder.

Mrs French was brought to trial at Lewes Assizes. The *Sussex Express* reported that she was pale with fear and had to be supported while in court. Villagers were stunned by the details of her trial. William Funnel, another farm labourer, said that on Christmas Eve French had been in high spirits and looked forward to a rarity in his home, an onion pie. When the two arrived at French's home, near The Gun Inn, he noticed that a young man named James Hickman was already there and that there was a certain coolness between French and the visitor. But French sat down to the hearty meal he had been anticipating with such relish. James Hickman gave evidence. He said he was aware French was very ill upstairs and his wife had told him his stomach was infected and that he had not long to live. Hickman said Mrs French's sister had left him for another man but the labourer's wife was plainly attracted to him – they had kissed together in the house on a number of occasions, he said. Once she had asked him if he would marry her if her husband was dead. His only reply was that he liked her 'very well'. Not long after that French was dead.

Evidence was then given that Mrs French had visited the house of a Mrs Crowhurst, the wife of a farrier at Horsebridge, where she asked for two pennyworth of arsenic because 'I am just over-run with mice'. Mrs Crowhurst prepared the arsenic and then wrote the word 'poison' on the packet. A statement by Mrs French was then read out in court, accusing Hickman of putting arsenic in her husband's onion pie. She added that Hickman had been in the house when the constable came to arrest her but he had hidden himself. She also claimed that when she complained of French staying out late at night, Hickman had said he had given him something which would 'make him stop out later'. But Mrs French's attempt to blame her husband's death on her former lover fell on deaf ears. The jury found her guilty of murder and the judge ordered her to be hanged.

The execution was one of the last public hangings to be witnessed at Lewes, and people flocked from far and wide to get a good view. A little before noon on April 17th, 1852, a crowd of almost four thousand people had assembled in North Street and Little East Street. At ten minutes to noon the death bell began to toll and the prisoner was brought out and led to the scaffold. Half way up the steps a white cap was fitted over her face. When she reached the top of the scaffold the cord was placed around her neck and the bolt of the trap was drawn.

Her body was cut down a few minutes later and buried in a lead coffin near the grave of Mary Ann Geering, the Guestling poisoner, within the outer walls of the prison.

All public executions were to cease in England within the next sixteen years, but the end of Sarah Ann French indicates that a revulsion was already setting in against a spectacle that 'had a brutalising effect on the public mind'. One eye witness later declared that on 'hundreds of faces in the crowd – and of youthful ones – we could only observe the smile of levity, or the callous laughter (sic) of recklessness. As for the moral lesson there was none; indeed, we are confident that it only requires the repetition of such scenes to render the effects of such an execution not only totally inoperative for good, but directly effective for evil.'

On a lighter note, one of the most popular dishes at The Six Bells in recent years was onion pies. Landlord Ken Boulter had toyed with the idea of naming them after the Chiddingly poisoner, but decided against it.